Testimonials

The subtitle to Madhava Dasa's book, **Flying With Angels GOD FIRST: Plant-Based Living In Love With God** caught my attention and for me links two ideas that are sometimes not linked together. In conjunction with heartfelt discussions about minimizing violence in eating in this world, it is vital to focus back on God's spiritual abode where peace reigns eternally supreme in contrast to this material world of endless quarrel and hypocrisy. ~ Gordon Stelter, Author and Pianist

I love the devotion that shines throughout this book about God and the conscious evolution to a healthy non-violent 100% vegetarian diet. ~ Torbin Hjorting, Retired Health Professional

Madhava Dasa's book **Flying With Angels GOD FIRST: Plant-Based Living In Love With God** is aptly titled because of the high and lofty ideas portrayed about God and a nonviolent conception of healthy plant-based eating. Due to the depth of the insights freely given, a second reading of the book yielded further understanding. ~ G. Giriraj Ramos, LA Metro Bus Operator and Suburban Poet

That God is compassionate and totally spiritual comes through loudly in this ultimately sweet book about God and healthy plant-based, nonviolent living in the here and now, while keeping focus on God's eternal beautiful existence. I always say, "Travel with God as your silent partner." God is portrayed in Madhava Dasa's book as *the* silent partner I want to travel with. ~ Ronny Jose Diaz, Author of: *Hispanic Heritage, My Journey From New Mexico To The Mountains Of Central America*

Madhava Dasa explains deep spiritual and philosophical ideas only a few pre-qualified persons will *immediately* comprehend to their full extent. I recommend thorough, thoughtful, repeated reading with a sympathetic open heart to discover the hidden treasure that lies within the pages of this greatly evolved work of a leading-edge and fearless thinker and aspiring devotee of our sweet Lord. ~ Eric Bott, Hawaii State High School history teacher

Flying With Angels
GOD FIRST

Plant-Based Living
In Love With God

By
MADHAVA DASA
of Maui

Transcendigital Productions

Copyright © 2022 by Madhava Dasa
810 Kelawea St Apt G3
Lahaina, Maui, Hawaii 96861
mdasa1@gmail.com
All rights reserved

Published by Transcendigital Productions
810 Kelawea St Apt G3
Lahaina, Maui, Hawaii 96861
808-878-6821

No part of this book may be used or reproduced in any manner without written permission from the publisher except for brief quotations in a review.

ISBN 978-0-9847258-1-6
Library of Congress Control Number: 2022907308
Printed in the U.S.

Contents

	Page
Preface	7
Introduction	7
Chapter 1 - God's Absolute Truth Defeats Death	11
Chapters 2 & 3 - How To Make God Happy	16
Chapter 4 - Who Does A Mother's Milk Belong To?	23
Chapter 5 - How Great Is God?	27
Chapter 6 - What Is "Life"?	32
Chapter 7 - God's Personal Supreme Transcendental Beauty & Glory	37
Chapter 8 - The Two Ideas That Make A Long Story Short	39
Chapter 9 - The Promise Of Peace	42
Chapter 10 - Pastor, Pope, And Guru	44
Chapter 11 - What Is This Place? What Is Love Of God?	47
Chapter 12 - Simple Explanation Of God Conscious Healthy Eating	50
Chapter 13 - The Shocking Truth About "Life"	54
Chapter 14 - Easy Way To Minimize Exploitation	59
Chapter 15 - Organic Revelation	61
Chapter 16 - God Is Eternity, And We Are Property - God's Property	64
Chapter 17 - What Are The Three Types Of Milk?	66
Chapter 18 - Why is God Free And Eternal?	68
Chapter 19 - Where East And West Agree	70
Chapter 20 - The Shocking Truth About Spiritual Ahimsa And Mundane Sustainability	72
Chapter 21 - Pandemic Of Half-Truth, And God's Full Stunning Beauty	75
Chapter 22 - What Is The Passage Back To God And What Is The Arrival?	78

Chapter 23 - How Do We Find Deep Peace Within Our-
            Selves & Only Think Of God's Happiness? 80
Chapter 24 - Without Freedom There Is No Divine Love 83
Chapter 25 - The Meaning Of Divine Love   85
Chapter 26 - What Does Abolitionist Vegan Mean?   88
Chapter 27 - If I Had The Wings Of An Angel   92
Chapter 28 - Lovingly Calling Out To God   94
Chapter 29 - Hidden Power Vs Innocent Surrender   100
Chapter 30 - How To Fall Into God's Loving Arms   102
Chapter 31 - Take The Good From The Left And
            The Right   105
Chapter 32 - "Real Religion Means Proper Adjustment" 109
Chapter 33 - Laugh, Laugh / No More Tears In Heaven 112
Chapter 34 - Science Devours Itself   114
Chapter 35 - One And A Half Gurus, And A Life Of
            Least Exploitation   116
Chapter 36 - Why We Should Love God Without Killing
            Or Stealing From Animals   119
Chapter 37 - Where Does Ecstasy Come From?   122
Chapter 38 - To WANT To Go Home   124
Chapter 39 - We Are Not These Bodies & Whole Food
            Vegan Is Crystal Clear   126
Chapter 40 - "The Free Flow Of The Absolute"   128
Chapter 41 - The Mother Of All Elephants In The Room
            And Where We Go From Here   130
Chapter 42 - Vegan Krishna, Or Krishna Vegan?   133
Chapter 43 - Krishna Vegan Is Evergreen   135
Chapter 44 - GOD FIRST Abolitionist Vegan   137
Chapter 45 - Duty To Serve God   139
Epilogue   141
Keyword Index   142
About The Author   143

Preface

While finishing up this book I was reminded of a phrase "...flying with angels" I wrote in one chapter. I saw that phrase and thought it would be a great title for the book. So to see how that phrase was used in the past I searched for it online. I thought there would be religious uses or something about the Blue Angels flight team, or maybe other book titles.

I live in Lahaina, Maui, Hawaii and do part-time street singing, and lo and behold the first results of the Google search were all of a Hawaiian song titled, "Flying With Angels". It is a beautiful song & I now sing it in my rotation of songs. A prominent background image in the online video when the song plays in the first Google result at the time of this writing, is a photo taken from the very beach that is closest to where my wife, Sunanda and I live. Out of 68,900,000 search results in the whole world, the first result was a song connected to a beach within walking distance of my residence, thousands of miles out in the middle of the vast Pacific Ocean.

Needless to say I took that as confirmation of the title of this humble book.

Introduction

This book is a compilation of short essays rendered as chapters, related to Eternal Beautiful God and to the ultimate elephant of all elephants in the material room. Some essays are directly to the point and some are auxiliary, but all contribute to the whole. This compilation book then ends with a summary epilogue, and a wish for humanity. Note: "Elephant in the room" means something so big you don't see it, or that you don't want to see it because it destroys your preconceived false narrative, so you ignore it.

How can we talk, or think of any PERFECTION of a societal (progressive, conservative, or whatever) utopia on Earth, when the big elephant in the room - unavoidable *killing to eat* - is negating and erasing EVERY aspiration for real goodness in this world.

This place, right here and right now, is the classic hell we imagine - the place of constant killing to exist by everyone, by every species.

BUT beyond the door and over the rainbow, there is a place without material killing. All the high concepts have, and must have an origin. They do exist, but they do not exist in reality in the material world. But they do beautifully exist in God's spiritual world. And that abode of God is not this material world, but is our destination AFTER we are released from this material prison where big mad elephants roam in the room.

And God's abode is so beautiful - so beautiful. And why is God's abode so beautiful? Because God is so beautiful!

By hearing from my Spiritual Master His Divine Grace Srila B.R. Sridhar Maharaj I understand that there exists power, consciousness, and superconsciousness. But mere, plain consciousness by itself is dry. Higher than power and consciousness is the NECESSITY of consciousness, which is beauty and ecstasy.

So when we speak of fulfillment and beauty we are looking for the *highest* concept of beauty in the Supreme Personality of God. God the father is great. God the son is great. God the merciful is great. But God the ALL-Attractive, is the greatest. God simultaneously at the CENTER of ALL loving relationships is greatest.

God in HIGHEST ECSTACY is the coming-of-age, teenage God, who lives village life in God's own transcendental beautiful rural nature, where playful God is the exclusive talk of the town, NOT in any limited lower mundane sense, but in the highest pure spiritual sense only possible with God proper.

All things good and bad are inconceivably harmonized in God. And being God, God can do anything and everything. But since WE are NOT God, but we are servants of God, we are only to do what God wants us to do. How are we to know what God wants us to do? Scripture, guru and saint POINT the direction, but the guru WITHIN is not to be neglected.

Eating entails disturbance to, stealing from, killing and grinding with our teeth, swallowing and passing out other fellow living entities. It's not that we have to stop eating, but to do that we will have to wait patiently until we are called home by God.

So we are going to the place where we don't kill to eat. And until God calls us home and gives us passage through the door and over the rainbow, if we are civilized, we are to live in this world following the full ahimsa vegan principle of doing the LEAST EXPLOITATION of others. And because daily eating is the primary activity in material life, that LEAST EXPLOITATION is premised on ahimsa, 100%

plant-based diet worship of God the ALL-ATTRACTIVE Personality.

A note here is that the name for God, Krishna, means "All-Attractive God". But as God is Absolute, *all* names for God are Absolute as names of God. So please, <u>no fighting about the particular name for God!</u>

In summary:
GOD IS ALL-ATTRACTIVE and

The ultimate elephant in the material room is:
KILLING TO MAINTAIN EXISTENCE

So, what to do?

Again, we are to worship God, and as the least exploitation while in this material world of constant killing, we are to follow a healthy whole-food vegan diet as per **Genesis 1.29, "I give you every herb and fruit bearing tree as your food." and Bhagavad Gita 9.26, "Offer me with love and devotion a leaf, a flower, fruit and water."** The plant-based diet is now also prescribed by the preponderance of modern scientific evidence. Full Circle. Can't you see it? Full Circle. God knows the past, present and future. Always did - always will.

Chapter 1
God's Absolute Truth Defeats Death

Greetings, my name is dasa (lower case), which means servant of God. This book is about God. Chapter 1 will introduce five of the major topics this book will investigate.

They are:
  1) God is eternity and we are property - God's property.
  2) God is Love and God doesn't kill unnecessarily (ahimsa).
  3) God owns everything and our proper enjoyment is to help God enjoy.
  4) We are not these bodies and material sense gratification ultimately leads nowhere.
  5) Death is the problem, and only death is the SOLUTION.

If you are interested in any of these topics go ahead and finish reading the book.

MOST RELIGIONS

How do most religions, religious teachers and gurus support themselves? That's easy to answer. They are salesmen, they are SELLING us the promise of our eternity. The preacher can't create eternity. God is eternity, and we are property (God's property), controlled by the whim of our Owner. We go to God and God does with us as God wishes, and God is infinitely free and unbound. Are we ready for that?

Look, God is free and unbound, otherwise God wouldn't be God. And we owe everything to God. We exist for God's pleasure and God is whimsical. God has that right, to be whimsical. God has all rights, we have none. We have no right including to eternity.

God will go on, that is the point of faith. If we love God, that is enough for us and we ourselves don't need eternity, because our beloved has it. And that gives us fulfillment.

So the first point is that God is Eternity and we are God's property.

The second point is, God is love and love doesn't kill unnecessarily. It is unnecessary to kill and eat *animals* for our best health. It's called a plant-based diet, and there's a preponderance of scientific evidence that supports that it is unnecessary to kill animals for optimum health. Like Tolstoy said, "A person can live and be healthy without killing animals for food; therefore if one eats meat they [selfishly] participate in taking animal life merely for the sake of their appetite [taste buds]."

Confusion is sown by vested interest or the ignorant when they use the extremities of the bell curve of evidence 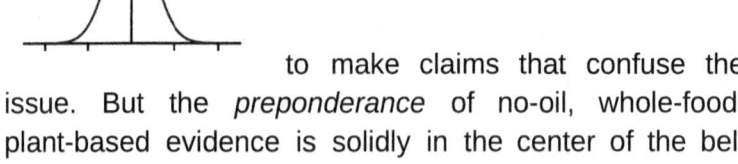 to make claims that confuse the issue. But the *preponderance* of no-oil, whole-food, plant-based evidence is solidly in the center of the bell curve, as opposed to the flared extreme edges.

The third theme is God owns everything and our proper enjoyment is to help God enjoy. In other words God is the Supreme Enjoyer, the proprietor of everything, and we are the multitude of servants.

13   Dasa/Flying With Angels

The best way to please God is to call out one of the many names for one of the many forms of the one Supreme Loving God. In this regard & related to point number two (ahimsa) is that in our _un_fallen state the one Supreme Loving God does not want us to kill animals as stated in Genesis 1.29 and Bhagavad Gita 9.26 [full quotes back on page 10]. Nor does the Buddha want us to kill animals in the Nirvana Sutra. Nor does plant-based science want us to kill animals. Please God by calling out God's name - and with ahimsa vegan plant-based offerings.

Again, God is the Supreme Enjoyer and it is our duty and pleasure to serve that one Supreme God of many names. The best way to please God is to call out or sing one of God's many names, just like when a little child calls out "mommy" or "daddy"; and to follow a plant-based vegan diet as requested by God.

The fourth topic is that we are not these bodies and sense gratification leads nowhere. The classic explanation is that we are the same person we were at birth, but that our bodies have changed, thus we are not this body. Because all bodies are doomed to perish, including the sun, and according to Scripture the universe, and our own particular material body, it's pointless to serve the body's whims, better to serve God's whims, better to face the music and focus our love on God, the only sure thing in eternity.

This is the point of faith: that God is eternal. As created beings, and not the Creator, we may or may not be anything according to God's will. Therefore focus on God and sing God's Holy Name. Offer God the type of food that God asks us to offer in the _un_fallen state. Namely a leaf, like kale or spinach; a flower, like Cauliflower and broccoli; fruits like tomatoes, eggplant, zucchini, bananas, and strawberries - it goes on and on. And of course clean fresh water.

Look, we wanted to be God, many still do, that's what this world is for, a playground for wasting time until we figure it out, "Oh darn, I guess I'm not God."

The goal is to develop our love for God. I mean gosh, God deserves our love. God has given us the *potential* to love God.

The fifth topic, and probably the most significant from our point of view, is that death is the only problem, and also death is the only solution. Birth, disease, and old age topped off by cold hard death, are the shallow surface problems. The deep underlying problem is the extension of topic two, which is that even if we don't kill animals unnecessarily for our appetites, we are still disturbing and killing and eating other non-animal living beings as if we were God and had that right.

Many say, "Of course we have that right, God told us we did." Well that's what the meat eaters say about *dominion* over animals, and that's what the vegans say about plants. Joaquin Phoenix, regardless of his politics, in his acceptance speech when he received his Academy Award for best actor, hinted at the real truth when he said, "We are talking about the fight against the belief that one nation, one people, one race, one gender, or ONE SPECIES has the right to dominate, control, use, and exploit another with impunity."

Even vegans kill to live. At the time of death we all need God's mercy. As every day killers, by what standard may we presume to live forever. By the standard of justice there is no way. Only by God's mercy can we hope to continue to serve the Lord after this body is no more. This book is a call for God's love and God's mercy upon us.

Death ends all killing, as Joaquin pointed to - all the exploitive killing of one species over another. What is called "sacred life" is merely the killing domination of one species over another. Only God has that right, and only God's life is actually sacred. This worldly life is only inappropriately justified killing. Thank God for our daily gluten-free-bread killing, all we want, but when push comes to shove, at the time of death, all our amens and prostrate obeisances won't cancel all our utterances of, "Wow, that was a good meal." And Lord Jesus Christ didn't die and resurrect for us to go on killing every day, and then get into heaven and go on killing.

This world is the hell of which we speak - really. Daily unending killing and exploitation of others. What gave the Kanamits the right to do what they did? Who are the Kanamits? They are the "heroes" of one of the most famous Twilight Zone episodes titled, *To Serve Man*. Go watch it - after reading this book. *To Serve Man. To Serve Man.* Simple title, *To Serve Man*.

On the surface death is the problem, but that's the shallow view. The deep view is that death is the *solution*. It's got to be a better place than this place of enjoying the taste of killing every day. But all is not doom and gloom. Remember God is Love, and God's Love is so sweet and glorious – a beautiful sunset, the rolling thunder, a majestic mountain, summer's cooling gentle breeze.

So there you have it, the outline of some major topics of this book, be sure to read it with great attention and reflection. You may not agree with every point in this book but the goal is to guide us in the right direction, as A. C. Bhaktivedanta said, "Back home, back to Godhead.

Chapters 2 and 3
How To Make God Happy

In the first chapter we outlined some of the major topics of this book which are:

1) God is eternity and we are property - God's property.
2) God is love and God doesn't kill unnecessarily (ahimsa).
3) Everything belongs to God and God is the Supreme Enjoyer. Our enjoyment is in serving God.
4) We are not these bodies and sense gratification ultimately leads nowhere.
5) Death is the only problem and death is the only solution.

In this chapter we will talk about how most everyone is secretly after power and position in this world, because down deep inside they know they are insignificant. It's okay, however, to be insignificant if all your energy is directed towards your Beloved, who is the Supreme Lord and is supremely significant and eternal. If you love God, God's beauty and eternality dominates your consciousness so completely that it doesn't matter if you are eternal or not, significant or not, because you rest in knowing your Beloved is the most significant and that God is eternal and blissful in ecstasy forever.

This material life, in our commonly conceived mistaken identity, is the battle to falsely prove how significant we are. But look at the universe, now look at yourself. We are insignificant. We think wealthy, powerful, famous and attractive people are the centers of interest, as if they were the most important things in the world. And yes materially they are important, but in eternal reality they are unimportant.

So we ourselves are mistakenly giving honor to material power and wealth, and to those who have successfully posed as significant. But only God has all power and all wealth, all fame, all beauty, all strength, all position, and all renunciation.

Now since time immemorial as soon as a baby pops out of the womb the baby is the center of our lives, and thankfully for us that's the way our mother felt about us. And therein is the dilemma. God or baby, and for some, it is God or dog. It takes a very strong person to renounce power, position, making babies, and worshiping dogs, and instead turn our consciousness to that of keeping God on our mind at all times.

We mistakenly take this temporary world as important and falsely think we can get some security here in this world. This world is only important as the opportunity to wake up from our slumber of dead-end sense gratification and our desire for our own happiness, and to turn to 24 hours a day serving God's happiness. Why God's happiness? Because we are headed for the grave, and God will go on. God is eternity and we are property, God's property.

Is God happy that we take our pet dogs or cats to the pet groomer regularly, and to the animal hospital for regular check-ups. All these things sound like great things to do, and they could be if you are now realized and you are living up to the responsibilities you took on before becoming realized. But are we doing these things for God's pleasure or for our own good feelings and pride of being a "nice person", and for our own mental feelings.

The point is, pride, power, and personal sense gratification always take away from the consciousness or mindfulness of the ultimate reality, namely that God is eternal and we are God's properties. God loves us, yes, but what are the activities of us loving God? Loving God is doing what God asks us to do whether directly in a broad way from Holy Scripture, or indirectly by scientific understanding of action and reaction in this world.

There are two things I can think of that God universally wants us to do to make God happy. The first is 24/7 calling out, singing, or thinking and remembering God's holy name, like a child calling out to their parents. And the second one is - as per Genesis 1.29 and Bhagavad Gita 9.26, and modern science - offering in a loving mood and eating a leaf, a flower, fruit, and pure, fresh water. No killing or exploitation of any animals.

Of course if you are shipwrecked on a desert island and there are no plants available and a chicken walks by, well hey, what to do? Sorry chicken, for making you the object of a joke. It hurts me to even do that. So I am deciding whether to keep this part in here or not. But we are talking about probably 99.9999 or even more of the time to be totally plant-based in our eating habits.

Calling out and or singing one of God's many names, and eating fruits and vegetables. Very, very simple requests. But who does it? Another point to remember is that the topics of this world, especially political ones, generally pull us away from thinking about God. Material topics and absorption in them can cloud our thinking and polarize it. Cloud it by overload with local time and place details, and polarize it by encouraging side-taking in the material world.

We then, are all the time focusing on temporary division and distribution of the resources of material nature. In other words using God's property for our sense gratification, as opposed to the investigation of the basic, deep, wide span, foundational issues, like the difference between a spiritual worldview, and a material one, and the degree of progress and direction on those paths.

Society should be set up for progress on the spiritual path. This world is no good, except as an opportunity to realize that it's no good. Why no good? Always killing, either plants and/or animals and too often babies in the womb.

Louis Armstrong sang a song, also covered by Izzy, "What A Wonderful World." The title sounds good but it is, and here's the kicker, just a plain whitewash of true reality, and another ignoring of the elephant in the room, which is daily, constant killing of one species over another. This constant killing is done without **deeply** acknowledging the utter self-promoting exploitation that is unapologetically engaged in while eating three times a day, 365 days a year. And then on Holy days, holidays, what do we do? Kill and celebrate by eating even more varieties of other living entities. Real Holy days would be fasting days.

But how is something like that going to happen? Well, man I don't know, but somehow can we honestly and openly admit how despicable we actually are, and acknowledge how our death is the only thing that will free us from our daily killing, and admit that our own natural death is a good thing. And then go ahead and eat to our body's satisfaction, acknowledging that we are not these bodies and we are trapped here by our own desire to be significant.

It doesn't matter bodily what race you are, whether you are on the left or the right, or whether you are a scientific globalist or a religious conservative, we are factually not these bodies that change from a baby body, to teenage body, to an adult body, and eventually to an old aged wrinkled body. But we are servants of God always.

All the body and country things are temporary. Fool, don't worship temporary things, and I'm talking to myself. This world is not only temporary, but equally important, it is also very nasty. Even the most pious saint is at least smashing, grinding and eating the most peaceful beings on Earth. The plants.

Plants may attack you over time if you move really, really, really, really slooowly. But generally plants are peaceful, quiet and well behaved, and we discount them despite their being children of God also. We discount that they have any right to exist, or if we verbally acknowledge their right to exist, we kill by eating them anyway without acknowledging in any deep way how nasty *we* are for doing that.

Acknowledging saints - you could say worshiping saints, it's like Hollywood praising themselves by giving themselves awards. There are no saints in this world, only killers. OK we are really going down a rabbit hole here. Lord please give me anyone who is an ahimsa abolitionist (see Chapter 26), plant-based vegan, AND who acknowledges that even a vegan saint is not a saint because they are still exploiting the plants. At least acknowledge that we are selfish killers of others and acknowledge that everyone just ignores their own despicableness, and acknowledge that there is nothing glorious and celebratory in eating, despite how many Hail Mary's or prostrate obeisances you throw out there.

The material world has to do with the left and the right, and how to divide up God's property for maximum dead-end sense gratification. The politically "left" worldview tends to be concerned with control in the name of equality in the here and now. This is sometimes called socialism or communism; or mayavad ("All people are one with, i.e., equal to God, therefore we are all God.") philosophy. And the "right" worldview tends to be toward freedom, self-control and eternal principles. Not that we become eternal, that's up to God, but we are satisfied to know God, our Beloved, is eternal and that's enough for us.

The right is somewhat more toward the spiritual worldview, but the right is also unfortunately, *very well mixed* with many worldly misconceptions. Either side can become perverted. Because either side can become perverted and misdirected, according to God in the Bhagavad Gita, God comes to this world or sends a representative periodically to straighten things out a bit. God tests us and offers us corrections, yes.

In the name of freedom and freedom's glory, which is love, God gives us choice on how to react to the tests. So choice and freedom are the gifts of God. Not freedom from duties of this world, but the freedom and choice to turn towards God and not to turn away. Love always requires freedom.

So all of the preceding statements taken together may have bogged-down one's mind by having included too many big words of heavy meaning. Simplicity - that which a child can easily understand is necessary, and here is that simplicity:

God is eternity and we are property, God's property. We exist for God's pleasure. God is free to do or change anything and everything in a moment's notice. God can destroy a universe in the blink of an eye, or conversely God can keep everything the same for eternity.

With that much (all) dependence on God we are mistaken to forget God even for a moment. The goal is to remember our destination, our Sweet Lord at all times and in all places, but we are the most fallen and can't remember God steadily for a day or even for an hour.

And now until next time may God show us Absolute Truth and Supreme Beauty. Thank you very much, por favor.

Chapter 4
Who Does A Mother's Milk Belong To?

Greetings my friends. We investigate spiritual topics about loving and worshiping God. Please read this chapter and this whole book to the end.

There are 5 main topics briefly discussed so far in chapters 1, 2 & 3 namely:

1. God is Eternity and we are property, God's property.
2. God is Love, and LOVE doesn't kill unnecessarily (ahimsa).
3. Everything belongs to God & God is the Supreme Enjoyer. Our enjoyment is in serving God.
4. We are not these bodies; therefore sense gratification ultimately leads nowhere.
5. Death is the only problem; and death is the only solution.

When will we make the decision to fully surrender to God and give up that last attachment to sense pleasure?

Go ahead and make a mental note of your biggest secret attachment, don't write it down, just a mental note. Is it an attachment you wouldn't want anyone else in the world to know? Is it? Good, that's the kind of attachment we are looking for.

Here's the goal - to trade that temporary attachment, for total devotion to Eternal God. The last straw, the last obstacle to freedom from matter, freedom from the chains of selfish sense gratification is to trade attachment to sense gratification, for attachment to God.

It may not be a secret attachment, but for some people their biggest attachment is milk, more specifically cheese.

Yes, that's right, cheese! Cheese is often one of the final attachments to selfish exploitation of God's beloved property. We'll come back to cheese in a quick moment.

The two greatest pure words in every language are: God, and Love. God is Supreme Masculine and Love is Supreme Feminine.

What is Supreme Masculine? Masculine likes to build protections. Masculine will sacrifice its life to protect Supreme Feminine, and Femininity relates to Masculinity through loving service. Supreme Feminine will sacrifice its life to serve Supreme Masculine. To protect and to serve. Great motto. Great life. Transcendental Life.

What is cheese? And why is cheese often the last material attachment to go in the opulent eating world?

Cheese is very concentrated milk, OK. So who does a mother's milk belong to? Does cow's milk belong to humans? Or does it belong to the mother cow and to her baby calf? To cow and calf.

If you say, we just take the extra milk, then what if Rod Serling's Kanamits from the Twilight Zone's program, To Serve Man, reappear and start taking half of all human mother's milk. What gives one species the right to exploit another? Is it simply power in the material world that makes for a perceived "right"? I think so.

So this so-called "sacred life" thing, is simply the power grab domination of the stronger over the weaker. And then the stronger ones write history in their favor, and attach "sacredness" to their actions.

Is this a heavy handed cynical description of material reality, or is it truth that sets us free? Free from our illusion of false self-nobleness and aggrandizement, no matter how "kind" we think we are. Freedom from false boasting of how significant we are, or of how surrendered we are, and how great we are. Krishna said water, not milk.

So back to cheese. Milk has a type of opioid in it, it keeps the baby feeding. Cheese concentrates that opioid, and presto, there's your addiction to cheese.

Other things are addictive also. How are we going to get away from those addictions? How do you break an addiction?

Well we've got to love something else, more than we love our addiction. In the case of cheese we have to value health and/or compassion and righteousness or pono in the Hawaiian language, above tongue taste.

Righteousness, virtue and decency. Great things, but if we are always killing plants and eating them, how are WE ever righteous, virtuous and decent?

The answer is that God, and only God, is Supremely righteous, virtuous and decent. If we truly love God we don't think about ourselves and our desires, we think about God's beauty and greatness. God's righteousness, virtue and decency. God asks us to be plant eaters only.

God is righteous, virtuous and decent. How so? God tolerates our weakness to remember God. Always waiting patiently on us to fully turn towards God and to focus on God. Focus, focus, focus on God.

So to FOCUS favorably on God, is the call.

Now because God is Infinite, how may little-we connect with God. To a little baby in a natural state, it connects with its mother initially by taking its mother's milk. After that the baby soon connects by uttering "Mommy, Mommy." That's how we connect with God. In times of trouble it's, "Oh my God, Oh my God." That's what we naturally say. "Oh mommy, mommy." "Oh my God, Oh my God."

Chant one of God's holy names regularly, aiming at 24 hours a day seven days a week. And eat what God asks us to offer to God in a loving mood, namely a leaf, a flower like cauliflower & broccoli, fruit & pure clean water.

That's about it for now. Until the next chapter, may God show you Supreme Beauty.

Chapter 5
How Great Is God?

This is chapter 5 in this book about God's Supreme Beauty and Flying With Angels.

Please forgive my repetition, I promise this will be the last listing of the 5 main topics of this book:

1. God is Eternity and we are property, God's property.
2. God is Love, and LOVE doesn't kill unnecessarily (ahimsa).
3. Everything belongs to God & God is the Supreme Enjoyer. Our enjoyment is in serving God.
4. We are not these bodies; therefore sense gratification ultimately leads nowhere.
5. Death is the only problem; and Death is the only solution.

Let's make some comments about each topic, one after another.

First - God is Eternity and we are property, God's property. **Sweet God has always existed and will always exist.** This is the basis of faith, the a priori knowledge that is independent of material experience. Faith.

We are created by God and are owned by God so we are God's property. Doesn't sound very romantic initially, but this is a difference between our relationship with God and our relationship with our parents for example.

God is unique and our relationship with God is like no other relationship. We are factually God's created property. We have no other foundation, support, or claim. Only that we belong to God. We don't belong to our parents, to our siblings, to our spouse, to our neighborhood, to our nation, to this planet, to this universe, or to Satan. We belong to God as God's created property, and God is Eternity. Our future or non-future is in God's hands – "He's got the whole world in His hands." Sing it.

If God wants us to be eternal, we are eternal. If God doesn't want us to be eternal we're not eternal. We can't project our feeble little ideas onto God. God is Absolutely Free, un-bound and unrestrained - except maybe by Love. But then again God is Love, don't forget.

Summing up the above: God is Eternity and we are God's property.

The second topic is as was just mentioned, God is Love, and LOVE doesn't kill unnecessarily.

It is not necessary to eat any animal products to have optimum, meaning perfect, health. There is just too much science, a preponderance of science supporting this fact. I mentioned the bell curve of evidence in a previous chapter and will in a future chapter.

A bell curve has the great preponderance of results in the central part of the bell, but there is always a flaring of outliers at each extremity. It is the extremities of the bell curve that are deviously, but perhaps occasionally innocently used to cloud, and confuse the issue of healthiest diet.

But the preponderance of evidence is for the plant-based vegan diet – which diet is related to the elephant in the material room. It's like in the covid-19, coronavirus pandemic the elephant in the room is the mistreatment of animals both domestic and wild. Eliminate the eating of animals, which is not in any way required for perfect health, and all natural pandemic viruses will be eliminated. To link to the science on that, search the term:

"Pandemics: History and Prevention" or "pandemic prevention: bird flu and emerging infectious diseases".

The third topic is everything belongs to God & God is the Supreme Enjoyer. Our enjoyment is in serving God.

Everything exists for God's enjoyment and happiness. If we deny this, that means we think this world is meant for OUR enjoyment. But that is a big mistake to think that way. Why is it a mistake? Simply because we must leave our body to be eaten by bugs and worms, ugh, or turned into burnt ashes. While God wins and goes on.

Our enjoyment is in serving God and knowing that regardless of what happens to us by God's desire, we may rest happy that God will go on. Beautiful God is everlasting. How great is that! How happy is that! What more could a lover of the Beloved unselfishly want, than that their Beloved should survive regardless of any thought of one's own self.

The fourth topic is: We are not these bodies; therefore sense gratification ultimately leads nowhere, just to suffering and ultimately to the grave.

Our fetus form of body is certainly not the present form of our body, nor is it our deathbed form. We can see, and we should hope, that we are not our body of flesh and decaying flesh. But we are the soul animating the body. When we leave our body it slowly rots or gets burned to ashes.

This business of sense gratification - enjoy, enjoy, enjoy - as the marketers say, doesn't end well. What are the lyrics to that song, "… the best you can hope for is to die in your sleep." But statistically our lives most often end with a sudden stabbing pain in the heart, or by slow starvation from universal inflammation caused by merciless metastasis of cancer, or by loss of consciousness from a muddied mind caused by Alzheimer's Disease, or by a myriad of other unpleasant endings.

Have you ever heard the quote: "The senses are a network of paths leading to death?" Well it's certainly true.

The fifth topic is: Death is the only problem; and Death is the only solution.

Death is the problem of the battle for existence. We can do pretty well in the early years of life but when the years progress to 70 or 80 one can easily see the big problem is, comin' round the bend.

You can exercise and eat right, watch your weight and don't do anything foolish, but that just really only delays the inevitable for a few more years - maybe.

There's nothing you can do to defeat death except to see it for what it is. What I'm going to tell you now you may have never heard before.

We always hear that life is sacred. Life is beautiful. Louis Armstrong's and Izzy's, "What A Wonderful World". Elton John's, "How Wonderful Life Is While You're In The World". It's all a lie. Not factual. Not true. A crock.

Killing and eating others 3 times a day is not a very sacred thing or beautiful thing to do. If you say plants and animals are not others, then what is to stop a race of superbeings from another planet from swooping in here one day and saying humans are not others. We see movies about it all the time. And you know if you see it in a movie it has got to be true. He said facetiously.

Really though, this place is a world where humans kill

animals to feed to their children, when the children naturally want only to cuddle the animals. How perverted.

Even abolitionist vegans of which I am one, kill plants endlessly. Killing, and then grinding them up with teeth that we spend thousands of dollars on to keep straight and shiny white, as if white teeth were a sign of purity or something.

So, far from death being something bad, actually our natural death is a good thing because it ends our killing of others on and on. Even if the soul is somehow eternal by nature and we are not killing the soul, only the body of another being, how is it that we can kill the body of and interrupt the existence of some other being on a daily basis on and on, and think we can get into heaven. By justice there is no way. Only by requesting mercy. When we give no mercy? Even if I cease to exist without a trace of being remembered I will fear no evil because I will have stopped my evil way of constant killing to eat that I am helpless to stop while I'm embodied with flesh and bone.

Will this view of things please God at the time of our death? I don't really think about that when I'm totally busy seeing the glory of God.

This song written by Carl Boberg comes to mind:

"O Lord, my God, when I in awesome wonder
Consider all the worlds Thy Hands have made

I see the stars, I hear the rolling thunder
Thy power throughout the universe displayed.

Then sings my soul, my Savior God, to Thee
How great Thou art, how great Thou art
Then sings my soul, my Savior God, to Thee
How great Thou art, how great Thou art."

Chapter 6
What Is "LIFE"?

Death is the perfection of life - thank you God.

From the philosophical left to the philosophical right: communist, socialist, liberal, middle of the road, conservative, libertarian, and even anarchist, all have the same underlying goal. What is that common underlying goal that unites all of these apparently divergent groups making them all effectively the same? They all want to personally succeed, and for their group to succeed and to live on in this world. Nobody wants to end their favored type of material existence.

Liberals generally prefer science to guide them on their journey, and conservatives prefer faith.

All true so far. But what they all want is for this same thing called "life" to continue on, at least for their own group.

We are proposing that ALL of them are equally wrong.

The keyword "life" is the main topic of this particular treatise. In other words, exactly what is life? Not what is consciousness, but simply what is life?

Now, love is the necessary second topic to life. Love is the highest thing. Love is higher than life. Some have sacrificed or given up their life for their love. Romeo and Juliet, Lord Jesus Christ, Chota Hari das. Love is the highest thing.

All is still true.

A starting question is: Who is included in your love? Is it only your own group? Remember we began by naming groups all the way from the far left to the far right. What about people in your "enemy" group? Remember, "Love" is the highest thing. Does your love include plants? Does your love include animals? Predator animals like dogs and cats? How about grazing animals like horses and little bunny rabbits? Why do people **not** eat dogs, cats, horses and bunny rabbits but **do** eat chickens, piggy's and cows? People cut up someone else's children and feed them to their own children or steal their milk or eggs. What the heck does "love" mean?

All this killing, points to the problem of this thing called "life".

Now, wait till you hear this:

This thing called "life", is demonic, or at least mistakenly thought of as a good thing. Why is "life" NOT a good thing? What is "loving" about killing others and eating them?

All so-called "life", basically sustains and continues by killing, feeding off of, and eating others.

God is All-Beauty, but this thing called "life" is factually hell. God allows this hellish life of our own device for killing and interference in the existence of others for personal temporary bodily sense gratification. Why did God create our situation? Because we selfishly & mistakenly want to enjoy ourselves independently of God, as if we were God. More about being equal to God coming up in a moment.

Now, one has to dive deep into seeing that this thing called "sacred life" is just the opposite of real life. This is the world of opposites. You think that the book *1984* is an opposite hell, well that ain't nothing compared to what this whole world thingy called "sacred life" really is.

(Except in an insignificant way only because we are insignificant parts of God) "Life" is more or less NOT sacred, because it has the backdrop of constant killing - animals and plants, the "enemy" in wars and too often babies in the womb. Only God is really fully Sacred.

No complicated explanations about how and why humans are so great & sacred, or some individual humans are "pure". Ok yes some humans are higher than others, but all are constantly killing and fall short of the glory of God. Still, thank you God for the saints throughout history.

Killing, killing, killing of others, typically known as breakfast, lunch and dinner.

But we say, "We have to eat to live"; or that, "Naturally we have to eat, so therefore there is nothing wrong with that." You say that humans killing plants is all right because, well, only humans can understand God and can think about God, therefore we are so great that all this killing doesn't matter and is not a fatal fault because we offer our killings to God. Bible followers have "dominion" over the animals, and vegetarians and vegans have the same attitude more or less over the plants.

"Life is sacred." "Life is sacred." "Life Is sacred." How often have you heard this? It's like, if you say something often enough then it must be true? No, life is killing and selfish interference - what is sacred about that?

And so many, when they say "life is sacred", they are only even thinking and meaning human beings. Again, their reasoning for thinking this way, their reasoning is that humans are so great because humans can think about and maybe understand God. As they go ahead just like everybody else, killing others all the time. And they do their killing as an offering to God saying that their offering foodstuffs to God is not killing because God purifies their nefarious act because of their preceptorial-line "surrendering" to God. Let them do that in peace because something is better than nothing. And I will continue doing that. But that doesn't change the fact that this thing called life is simply continuous killing, on, and on, and on, and on. Until saving death do us part from all this constant killing.

Ok, if we want to continue on in our present material body,

we do have to kill and eat. Eating only leaves and fruit that fall off trees is not good enough to avoid killing because by walking over to the tree you are crushing insects who also value their lives just like you do.

So, what are we to do? Go ahead, keep on killing and eating and be AWARE, i.e. CONSCIOUS or MINDFUL that our personal natural death is the ONLY solution to the problem of reaction to constant killing (not our offerings of our killings in the name of God, but only our concrete death that stops all killing) and be aware therefore that "Death is The Perfection of So-Called Life." And even if the soul is not killed when we kill and eat other's bodies, our glorious death at least stops our extreme interference in the existence of others. Exactly how, as constant killers, are we that great that our actions benefit the spiritual progress of slaughtered and mistreated others. More self-aggrandizement.

So where is meaning in all this? The meaning is that all meaning is in God, that is the point. God the Supreme Person is our goal, God is our destination, and God is our everything. And access to God is through surrender and constant contact by uttering and actively remembering God's Holy Name always and never forgetting God even for a second.

The next chapter after this one will be directly about God's Supreme Transcendental Beauty and Glory.

Okay, all the ideas of the political spectrum from the extreme left through the center to the extreme right are misguided in as much as they base everything on the continuation of "killing-life", through **domination** of their own ideas, combined with **production** of children who also kill to live - towards the goal of perpetuating the thing called "life", thinking it is so great. But not realizing that so-called life, the thing called life, is simply killing - on and on and on and on. Material life is an insignificant, tiny point of constant killing, and we make such a big deal about it, we actually worship its continuation. Not.

We are not worshiping God, we are actually worshiping killing.

Is all the aforementioned too much and too negative and cynical? Yes it is, because that is the negative side, the dark side.

But now as George Harrison said, "Here comes the sun"...

Divine Love though, is a horse of a different color. Divine Love is infinite. True Love, not this material world of killing, is transcendental, beyond this material world of daily killing that we are helpless to stop except by the death of our material body. Die to live.

God is Great and All-attractive. All glories to our natural realized death. Ki Jai and Amen.

And now until next chapter - May God show us Absolute Truth and Supreme Beauty. Thank you very much, por favor.

Chapter 7
God's Personal Supreme Transcendental Beauty And Glory

Many have glorified God throughout human history. It's easy to speak and write about the glory of God but more difficult to follow even God's basic instructions. God's original and basic instruction in eating hardly anyone follows. We are not talking about the largely symbolic fruit of the tree of the knowledge of good and evil. But of God's direct simple instruction on exactly what to eat, which is effectively the same in both Genesis 1:29 and Bhagavad Gita 9.26.

This situation points to one of the great glories of God, and that is that God gives us free will to obey or not to obey. God is Love, and through God-given infinitesimal free will, God facilitates loving reciprocal relationship with God. Without free-will there cannot be love.

This to obey or not to obey, free-will love arrangement is transcendentally beautiful and is a main glory of Godhead, summarized in the statement," Divine Love is a free-will transaction."

And true love for God is selfless, whereby the lover becomes unconcerned with their own existence, being totally absorbed in pleasing their Transcendental Beloved.

The ULTIMATE glory of God, is that God is totally free and unbound. Everything that exists, exists with or within God, and God can change anything and everything in a flash, or not change anything and everything for eternity. But we cannot second-guess God and we are totally, really totally, dependent upon God's sweet will, God's whimsical sweet will.

I have heard from my teacher Srila B. R. Shridhar that even though God said something in Scripture, that something is subject to change by God. God is free to act and is not bound by any rule or law. Otherwise God is not God. The specific case is that the soul is described as eternal in Bhagavad Gita and many other places, and it was pointed out that God who is free and unbound could actually even efface the existence of any particular soul or the whole class of created infinitesimal souls. Efface means to erase without a memory or trace of ever having existed.

Some may think this is an indication of God's power, but some may feel this is an aspect of God's pure beauty. If you rightly feel small, and are trying to fall in love with God, then the Absolute Unlimited Power of God could be seen as a beautiful thing. Whether power or beauty, certainly God is glorious.

The fact of God's freedom and unboundness i.e., God can be anything God wants to be; leads to God's Holy Name as being the only sure truth in eternity. Thus the utterance and remembrance of a name for Holy God is everything.

Because we are embodied as constant killers, all glories to our natural realized death. Ki Jai and Amen.

And now until next time may God show us Absolute Truth and Supreme Beauty. Thank you very much, por favor.

Chapter 8
The Two Ideas That Make A Long Story Short

Where do I begin? Let's begin with the conclusion and then jump back to the very beginning. The conclusion is that both the same God in Genesis and the same God in Bhagavad Gita want us to be healthy, loving 100% plant-based vegans *and* worshipers of God.

In today's world, more persons on the political left are vegans than on the right, BUT many persons on the left are either declared or functional atheists. Still, many on the left and most on the right practice fatal domination over innocent grazing animals while keeping meat-eating animals like cats and dogs as pets. One would think there should be some kind of cognitive dissonance maybe? Love your neighbor and your cat and dog, but kill the innocent grazing animals? At the very least it is a mean existence.

The objection is always that, "Well you vegans and vegetarians kill the plants." Ahh, and yes this is a valid statement.

Here's the thing that nobody wants to hear: this world is not the wonderful place full of love and beautiful sunsets that everyone says it is. What it is, is the place of killing. As said before in a previous chapter, "Killing, killing, killing - otherwise known as breakfast, lunch and dinner." We kill plants and animals and always each other in endless wars over time, and then poets praise this place, "And I say to myself, 'What a wonderful world'." Everyone it seems has something to sell you.

So, the problem is to be BOTH a worshiper of God *AND* a loving vegan. One might say, in other words, to be a true worshiper of God according to God's original request in both the Christian Scripture and the Hindu Scripture.

Maybe both the democrat atheist vegans, and the heartless "theist" republicans are cursed. And if you look at today's present world here today you can see that both sides are cursed in some way or the other.

So there has got to be a **THIRD WAY** beyond this world's left & right polarities, there's got to be a morning after. And there is - but that way will never be in this world, because this world is the world of endless killing. We have got to get out of this place, we have to want to get out of this place. We have to see this place for what it is and have nothing to do with it, at least mentally.

Everything belongs to God, everything.

Now as promised will we jump back to the beginning:

God said in Genesis 1.29, "I give you every herb and fruit bearing tree as your food." And the same God also says in Bhagavad Gita 9.26, "Offer me with love and devotion a leaf, a flower, fruit and water."

In Christian terminology the "knowledge of good and evil" in the Garden of Eden, *THAT* is the entrance by the devil's half-truth, is the entrance or appearance in this world of the illusion that we are equal to God, also known as oneness with God. In other words the phrase, "Knowledge of good and evil" means being equal with God, and therefore everything is equal. Or that everything should be equal. Oneness with God and "equality" or "equity" are the same idea, the same mistaken negatively reactive idea exposed in the Christian version by eating the symbolic fruit of the tree of the knowledge of good and evil; and in Bhagavad Gita simply by refusing to surrender to God as the Original Supreme Factual Person of Unlimited Beauty.

1. That this place is **not** our home in any way shape or form, except as a place to realize that this is **not** what we want; that this place is **not** our true home, and 2. That while we are here we should do the minimum killing and exploitation of animals, via observing the scripturally prescribed plant-based vegan diet of fruits and vegetables.

These are two main ideas to be embraced as souls surrendered to God the Supreme Beautiful Person:

1. This place of kill-to-live is **not** our home, and
2. Scripture (even science) prescribes a plant-based vegan diet of fruits & vegetables while we are here.

Oh, and the ultimate point is that there is a way of being, beyond the left and right of this world. That way of being is that, because God is absolutely free and unbound, nothing is sure in this world or in the Spiritual World except that there is a name for God, the Original Free and Unlimited Person.

Uttering and always remembering and never forgetting a name for Holy God is the third way of being, the way of being that leads us out of this hell of constant killing-to-eat that we are living in.

Die to live.

All glories to our natural realized death because that ends all killing and exploitation. Ki Jai and Amen. And now until the next chapter, may God show us Absolute Truth and Supreme Beauty.

Be thankful very much, por favor.

Chapter 9
The Promise Of Peace

Back to Godhead, back to Eden.

Please understand that all the ideas presented in this book are subject to change and further understanding, and that these ideas are here simply to get us to focus on and think about God & the Absolute Truth.

I was first attracted to God consciousness during the Vietnam war when I saw on TV, at the large famous Washington, D.C. antiwar protest of 1969, I saw a third group wearing orange robes with bald heads and ponytails dancing and chanting. I immediately sensed that this third group, at that time, was neither left nor right, but beyond.

God is great. A child can understand this. Anyone can understand that SOMEONE made, for example, a watch - and that the watch did not assemble itself and happen accidentally, no matter how many times you throw a handful of dirt and rocks on a table. In the same way one can understand that the universe and the wonders of the universe are not accidental. So simple to understand.

Actually there is nothing totally, fundamentally new to add to any religious tradition. But merely a further development, an adjustment, a tweak so-to-speak, to the set of basic universal theistic ideas, namely mercy, harmony, sweetness, beauty, and so forth. Specifically in this case, to healthfully minimizing the exploitation inherent in the thing called "life".

Genesis 1.29 and Bhagavad Gita 9.26 both prescribe an animal-free diet. The preponderance of modern scientific evidence leads to a plant-based diet. The central part of the bell curve of scientific evidence, yields an animal-free diet, and a diet free of all separated oils. No, you don't need separated oil's to grease your joints, actually those oils clog your joints. This oil-free thing is not as harsh and austere as one initially may fear. Briefly, one simply substitutes plant-based, whole-food, oily-seed-spices in cooking, like whole or whole powdered cumin, fennel, mustard, fenugreek, black pepper and more. You get the idea - and you get the taste, without the disease. No separated oil.

Once you learn a few basic things it's actually very easy to prepare and cook nice tasting dishes to offer to our Great and Beautiful God.

The only thing that really prevents us from making good progress is attachment. Attachment to past habits, attachment to pre-existing traditions, and attachment to other people that maintain the old, and especially in regard to the animal-free part, cruel practices that are not necessary in the modern technologically advanced world full of supermarkets.

So let's really go back home, back to Godhead, back to Eden and back to what Lord Krishna and Genesis actually ask us to offer with love - a leaf, a flower, fruit and water.

Many progressive scientific lefties get the animal-free part of the equation, but because many of them are abortionists, they fail the test. Right wingers tend to worship God, but too many of them are too-proud animal killers, they also fail the test.

It's time to make a little adjustment to fulfill the promise of peace posed in 1969 by the little band of monks I saw in Washington, D.C.

And now may God show us Absolute Truth And Beauty.

Chapter 10
Pastor, Pope and Guru

Because God is free and unbound, all ideas are subject to change and further understanding, here in this book and throughout the universe.

In this world, by the Lord's arrangement, it's all about name and fame, power and position. And by God's arrangement, who has the most name and fame? Well that would be God.

Power, who has the most power? Again that would be God, obviously. But now, power and position in this world is what people are after. And power in this world is related to name and fame, and income stream.

In whatever world - people are attracted to those with power, name, and fame. It's like a social proof. In the material world, society consciousness, also known as group consciousness, is predominant. But in the spiritual world, in Bhagavad Gita 18.66 God ultimately says, "Abandon all varieties of religion and surrender individually directly to me." No societies. This does not mean though, that spiritual societies are not beneficial in their time and place, but that they are not ultimate.

In Jesus's time the Sadducees had the power of being controllers of the main temple in Jerusalem. Jesus did not like that the Temple was being used for economic profit by selling Passover sacrificial doves and running money changing operations. When Jesus overturned the money changer's tables inside the temple, and said "God's house is a house of worship not of business", well what did that threaten - the temple leader's income stream; thereby threatening their position of power - and around it goes.

Lord Jesus was hung on a cross only four (4) days after this incident.

It threatened the money, and the power of one of the established groups of power at that time.

The lesson is that if you threaten someone's income stream they don't like it and they don't like you. Imagine a non-politician running for a big political office. At first the political and economic power establishment will ignore and laugh at you until you get some traction or backing, and once you get that, they will attack you. In Jesus's case, he paid the ultimate price only four days after disrupting things in the Temple. This is one of the major sins for which Jesus died to point out to us. To point out in the ultimately dramatic way, to make broadly public the story that God's house is not a house of business but of worship and of how disrupting the income stream of those with power, can cause a violent reaction. Jesus made the point that God comes first, and not our position of power supported with an established income stream. Die to live.

A best selling author named Dr. Will Tuttle wrote an article about why no spiritual teachers, pastors, popes or gurus are preaching an animal-free, sometimes known as vegan, diet. In that article Dr. Tuttle said that a critical mass of vegans is necessary first before a vegan-preaching religious leader or guru can appear.

That is because there would not be enough of an income stream to support, in any large way, that particular pastor, pope, or guru. No money, no power.

The subconscious, or conscious thought of losing funding, blinds many established leaders to making forward progress in the evolution of consciousness. For those who already have a reliable income source that backs their position of power, to lose that source is a fate they refuse to accept, at the expense of actually making spiritual progress. Loose money-source, loose power. Power and a comfortable position is the most intoxicating thing. Withdrawal is tough.

So those with the strength to do it, must withdraw as much as possible from the world of power jockeys and world news. Because power jockeys seldom get off their power trip horses and because the world of quarrel and hypocrisy cannot be cured, we have to withdraw ourselves as much as possible from the whole material conception. What one group sees as light, the other group sees as darkness, is really true and not just a poetic proclamation.

Helplessness in front of God is reality, and die-to-live in love of God by always remembering God and never forgetting God is the solution.

Well that's about it........ peace.

May God show us Absolute Truth and Supreme Beauty.

Thank you very much.

Chapter 11
What Is This Place? What Is Love Of God? And The Wish For Everyone

What is this place, that really is the question. The whole thing is prefaced on learning to see what this place actually is. You must be able to accurately describe this world in a tweet or two. And here it is:

"This place is a collection of individuals that eat other individuals. One of these broad groups of individuals, called humans, think they are more valuable than any other group and therefore they could be called human supremacists. Within that human supremacist group are subgroups that continuously battle each other for ultimate supremacy. They are all generally called left & right. Unfortunately however, 'The paths of glory lead, but to the grave'." - MD

What is 100 years within an infinite number of years? Nothing. So ultimately we are nothing, this place is nothing. The material family world is all about the struggle to falsely claim that we are something. Two of the main claims of humans are that 1) We have intelligence superior to other species, animals or plants, therefore we are great, and 2) We are the only group of entities that can inquire or think about God, therefore again we are the greatest thing since sliced bread.

Flying to the stars with the scientists, or worshiping God with the theists, we are all headed to the grave. The moon flyers think we will keep flying from planet to planet and that at some point along the way, we will figure out how to pause aging forever. Most God preachers sell us the promise of our eternity after death, "just follow me and our group, and you will get eternal life."

Nothing wrong with eternal life, per se, but having that desire for one's own self or for one's extended family or nation's self, perfectly fits the definition of what selfishness is. In material life one individual constantly eats other individuals, and then we want eternal existence after that, taking help of whatever savior is available.

What about God's happiness and the investigation into that? What about loving God so much that we forget about our own happiness and our own everlasting life? What about unselfishness after death, for a change, in place of the continuation of material life's selfishness of always eating others 3 three times a day - eating others being one of our main activities of happiness…and enjoying the "taste" of it?

Love is a common word. Love, love, love that's all we hear about - how great love is. Love is toward someone else. And all that is well enough, but the problem with material love, as opposed to Spiritual Love is that this here-and-now stuff is all temporary and headed for the grave. Material love of family and of our personal activities is no good, in that it may not transfer over after death.

But God goes on. God goes on. If you think otherwise you're classed as an atheist. Anything and everything is possible for God. God has all everything. All love, all power, all beauty et cetera.

Love of God should be our all-consuming activity, but who accomplishes that?

Certainly not myself - but it is possible that someone somewhere has done that. Considering the multitudes of people coming and going, over multiple thousands of years on this planet, there may have been at least one, and if there was one, there may have been many.

Anyway our task now is to love God to the extent that we forget so much about ourselves, and only hunger, not for our next meal, but for our Eternal Beloved Lord's happiness.

Above all else may you, and all of us, learn how to deeply love God and give up our own petty selfishness.

Thank you very much.

Chapter 12
Simple Explanation Of
God Conscious Healthy Eating

This chapter is about the simple explanation of healthy eating, and how to make the change.

In the material world energy comes from the sun. Sunlight hits the leaves of plants and that is where healthy eating starts. With the leaves of the plants. All protein on this planet is originally made in the leaves.

Leaves have the highest percentage of calories as protein. Animals only rearrange the protein that they take in, that originates from the leaves. As far as the plant goes, the leaf's function is to gather energy, ultimately for the plant's reproduction. Reproduction via the seeds.

The further along in its life cycle that the plant develops, the more calories are concentrated in its new reproductive parts and the lower the nutrient density becomes in each succeeding part.

The highest nutrient density, in other words the highest nutrients per calorie, not nutrients per gram or per serving size, but per calorie, is created in and present in the leaves. Nutrients per gram or per serving size, belong in the trash bin of wrong ideas just like the flat earth idea of planet Earth. The per calorie view of nutrition is the only correct idea of nutrition, just like the spherical (slightly pear shaped) Earth is the only correct idea of the shape of the Earth.

In this technologically advanced age, availability of too-high, calorie-dense foods is widespread, whereas our bodies are not accustomed to a steady diet of these high calorie-dense foods. And whether one is fat or thin on the outside, one can in effect be fat on the inside, especially on the inside of the blood vessels.

By Almighty God's, or at least by nature's arrangement, the healthfulness of food via nutrient density begins at its highest point with the leaf and then healthiness decreases through the remainder of the plant's reproductive life cycle as it gathers more and more calorie density.

What appears in the plant life cycle after the leaf? That would be the bud of the flower such as broccoli, artichoke and cauliflower. Then the flower bud blooms into petals, where for example, rose petals are edible and healthy food, although generally people aren't eating so many actual flowers in the technologically advanced countries.

Next the flower produces the fruit including vegetable fruits like green beans, okra, eggplant, cucumber and so forth. And then there are all the regular sweet fruits.

The fruits contain and produce the seeds. Grains are simply grass seeds. All seeds, by being further along in the growth cycle of the plant have less and less nutrients per calorie density.

The grazing animals eat the grass and grass seeds and produce muscle, bone, gristle, brains, tongues, and blood, most of which doesn't even sound appetizing. As far as your healthy blood vessels go, animal products in the modern age of easy availability, are stone cold killers of humans. What to speak of the mass imprisonment and killing of the animals.

So there is a regression of healthy eating from leaf, to bud, to flower, to fruit and to seed. Other than whole-food natural plant-parts - processed, fractionated, concentrated plant foods, and all animal source foods produce early and chronic debilitating diseases.

The way to make the first big change in improving our diet and health is to have a little sympathy for the poor, docile grazing animals, and to stop killing and eating them, including stealing chicken's eggs and in the case of cows, their milk which belongs to their babies.

The second big change is to substitute high taste, whole spices and whole ground spices like cumin, coriander, sesame seeds, etc., in all cooked and baked preparations, in place of all separated oils including canola & olive oil.

Contrary to the thought that we need to eat separated oils to grease our joints, separated oils simply clog our blood vessels and even our individual cells, causing in the case of clogged blood vessels all the cardiovascular diseases like heart attack, stroke and Alzheimer's, and in the case of oil-clogged individual body cells, causing along with sugar, and animal products, the diabetes epidemic the developed world is suffering.

In summary, because of decreasing nutrient density, healthfulness begins highest with the leaf, and follows downward the life cycle of the plant. And then goes negative with processed foods and all animal products.

Permanent positive change in your diet and health is most easily effected by having sympathy, and a non-intervention policy for the poor grazing animals and including fish. And by replacing separated oils with whole and ground seed spices.

All this type of eating still involves disturbing and killing plants, and the best we can do is to prepare the plants as humble offerings for the Lord with love and devotion for the Lord's pleasure, not for our sense enjoyment.

Offerings of whole non-animal foodstuffs to the Lord are temporary reprieves from the penalty for sin. Our death is the only possible permanent cessation of our sins of disturbing and killing and eating other entities that value their own lives as much as we value ours.

And now until next chapter may God show us Absolute Truth and Supreme Beauty. Thank you very much.

Chapter 13
The Shocking Truth About "LIFE"

What is the one topic above all other topics? Remember the song with the lyrics, "Love is a many splendored thing."? A beautiful line from an old materially beautiful song.

Unfortunately that is not our topic today. We are all going to die. Now many of you will instantly turn your face, because the material world wants us to think death is a bad thing, that death is a bad word. Why does the material world want us to think that? So they can keep on selling us unnecessary items for temporary bodily sense gratification generation after generation.

But what if we thought of the word death as we think of the word love, beauty or even fame, power, or money.

In the book *1984* by George Orwell, in the language Newspeak, Ingsoc stands for English socialism, and the name of the totalitarian ruling party of Oceania, is "Big brother", the ostensible purported leader of Ingsoc.

Big brother's philosophy is summed up in the slogan: War is peace, freedom is slavery, ignorance is strength. Just the opposite of the true meanings of the words. In this world it's the same with the words "birth" and "death". The true meaning of these words in the material world is the opposite of the real meaning.

What do we commonly hear, "Oh how wonderful, beautiful and miraculous birth is", and the other word death is commonly known as the grim reaper, never the happy reaper.

55   Dasa/Flying With Angels

Let's look at the true vision of what is going on in the material world. And what might that be? Killing, endless killing at least three times a day, called breakfast, lunch and dinner. And forever repeating wars.

Only by assigning mystic superiority to the human species may one view birth into this world as a wonderful thing. "Oh the animals are such brute savages. Their killing of each other is pure savagery."

Whereas our killing is only a necessity, or even worse than that, our killing is thought of as a divine right. Some will say, "I don't want to hear all this talk of death, all this negative scary stuff." Some will also say, "Why are you harping on this terrible word death." But man the thing is, the word death, is not the bad thing it's made out to be. And the word life is not the great thing it's made out to be.

Can you believe that death is the best thing, "...the passage back to the place I was before", like the phrase the Eagles used. And another phrase that we heard from Shrila Prabhupada, founder of the Krishna Consciousness movement in the West, namely Back home, back to Godhead. Death is the wonderful miraculous thing that ends all worldly domination, exploitation, disturbance and killing and eating of other co-equal living entities, spiritually co-equal living entities.

There's another thing, another idea of the Oceana type material world, namely that humans are superior and we are not spiritually co-equal with animals, with plants, or with bugs. "No, we are the greatest. We are humble. We have saints and skyscrapers. What have amoebas done lately? Have they flown to the Moon.? Have they built Twin Towers? Have they developed vaccines to protect themselves from self-inflicted diseases?"

Look at the world now and this covid-19 BS (please pardon using the abbreviation). Hold on for a second and you'll know what I mean by the term BS in a short moment. Not that covid-19 is not real. Now, at the time of this writing the endless question is to vaccinate or not to vaccinate?

Another current topic is: "Is this a ruthless takeover by the power elite of our individual freedoms, or is it the benevolent response of superior intellect to protecting the citizens of the world from dastardly disease?"

Again it seems the group the Eagles in the Hotel California song also hit on the dilemma of this material existence, and that is that we can check out any time we like, but we can never leave.

Those *excessing* on either side of the covid-19 debate are foolish (but this does not mean the virus is not real or that we should not take precautions). They're all missing the scientifically documented but ignored fact, that virus pandemics are a reaction to the, as it turns out unnecessary (although we didn't know this before, we do know it now), exploitation of mostly docile grazing animals (and possibly crazy scientist's gain of function research).

To link to a mainline hour long video on the science of virus origins and pandemics being linked to domestication of animals - search the term: "Pandemics: History and Prevention" or " pandemic prevention: bird flu and emerging infectious diseases". What we do know now is that the recent uptick in the number of pandemics is a reaction to the enslavement of and crowded conditions of factory farmed animals, and the eating of wild animals especially in a particular large country in Asia but also in other countries.

57   Dasa/Flying With Angels

In the video that you will find when you search the aforementioned phrases, you will see that pandemics in human history appeared only after domestication of formerly wild animals. Look it up, all these pandemics and communicable diseases are crossover diseases from animals, except maybe for any man-made viruses, lab created by Hitler-like crazy scientists.

The truth is pandemic diseases, for example chickenpox, are guess what - coming from chickens. Specifically close association with large compacted concentrations of animals.

Pretty soon they will be making chickens wear masks and staying 6 feet away from everybody. And that might be okay as long as we don't kill and eat them or keep stealing their eggs, which come out in the modified chicken version of a mammalian menstrual cycle.

Why not set the chickens free. Stop killing and eating them.

We didn't know this stuff in the past, but we do now, and it is so conveniently being ignored. Why? Because this world is hell. The penalty for sin is birth into this world, not death. Natural death is the beautiful thing and truth that will set you free. But because of the material world's 1984 type reversed thoughts of birth and death, because they are so ingrained in our consciousness and in the whole material existence, we can't easily see this. Death, and I'll say it again death, and one more time death, death, death, death, maybe that was four more times. It's not the end of life, it's the end of killing, and that BIRTH is the ENTRANCE INTO HELL.

So what to do? First try to remember that every political topic of the world is about keeping us within the material world of constant killing by eating. Progressives, conservative Patriots, social activists, they all talk a good talk, very interesting and inspiring. But it is all within the framework of the material world, which ignores, as we said, that the material world is a killing field.

All these causes left, right, globalist, patriot, simply want to perpetuate the material world. It sounds like a good thing, but it's not. And people want to argue, "Oh it's beautiful, look at that sunset", and "Oh the baby, look at the baby smiling." What does the baby do, start screaming and demanding food and you're forced to like it.

Practically speaking, individually what should we do to try to minimize our constant killing? We do this by adopting a healthy, totally plant-based diet offered to the Lord in a surrendered mood just as God asked of us in the unfallen state in both Genesis 1.29 and Bhagavad Gita 9.26.

And always remember this world is only for our temporary internment. And especially always remember to lovingly always call out one of God's Holy Names, constantly.

Now please don't take the following in a wrong lower way but in the highest possible spiritual way, from the song, "Once On A High And Windy Hill" taken as being about God, and a lost but now found fallen soul.

"In the morning mist two lovers kissed and the world stood still.
Then your fingers touched my silent heart and taught it how to sing.
Yes, true love's a many splendored thing."

And now may God show us the Absolute Truth and Supreme Beauty. Thank you very much.

Chapter 14
Easy Way To Minimize Exploitation:
Wings of an Angel and the Flight of the Eagle

"Oh if I had the wings of an Angel, over these prison walls I would fly", that was from the song titled "The Prisoner's Song", sung by Louis Armstrong. Louise's song addresses our greater situation, namely that, as the musical group the Eagles wrote, "Your prison is walking through this world all alone."

The greater situation is that we are caught in an imprisoned situation. The idea of any permanent future Utopia in this world is insanity. The idea that this world and our present material body is a prison is not new. Then there's that other song that says, "The world is a ghetto."

Whether prison or ghetto, we are in a dire situation, which is bottom line, really a killing field of breakfast, lunch and dinner, aborted babies and continuously reoccurring wars egged on by egomaniacal political and munition manufacturing leaders.

Generally though, throughout history we also have various religious personalities and philosophical texts that try to explain the world and how to get out of it.

Jaddu Krishnamurti, an Indian spiritual teacher wrote a book titled, *The Flight of the Eagle*, where the title, *The Flight of the Eagle* continues on inside the book to say, "...that does not leave a mark."

The analogy or reference to the flight of the eagle is that when the eagle soars through the sky, there's no apparent disturbance in its wake.

So just outlined here, is our predicament, and what we should do while in this prison. Using the wings of an angel or an eagle, we should minimize exploitation while we are materially embodied, and when the time comes simply fly away from this world of birth and death back home, back to Godhead. No more killing, exploitation or disturbance.

Part of the problem is that the material world does not want us to minimize exploitation. The mistaken consciousness of the world's cadre of co-conspirators actually wants us to *maximize* exploitation. That is a problem, at least part of the problem.

The idea to help us get out of this world of exploitation is to do the least exploitation while remembering God.

Beyond not creating babies and unnecessarily engaging in unjust wars, let it be known here that stopping very bad guys like Hitler, in a war, is not unjust. Meaning that there are some few defensively entered wars that are justified. But most wars are unjustified.

Anyway the idea to help us get out of this world of exploitation is to do the least exploitation. Easily doable on a simple daily basis is to offer to the Lord, and to eat a diet that minimizes the (totally unnecessary for optimum health) vulgar exploitation of animals. God asked us to do this in both Genesis 1:29 and Bhagavad Gita 9:26.

Just see the animals as your brothers and sisters, "Come on people now smile on your brother everybody get together try to love one another right now, right now."

May God show us the Absolute Truth and Supreme beauty. Thank you very much.

Chapter 15
Organic Revelation

There are many plant-based, vegan people who want to serve God. First of all, I must say I love you, because you make me feel happy, and you give me hope.

There are many names for God and God is Loving. That is for sure. It's a little rare to find people who want to love and serve God **and** who understand that we share a common conscious existence with animals. In the spirit of freedom, ahimsa, and giving honor to others, to claim ownership of and to restrict the free life of any animal is pure species bigotry.

Let's go higher. We are social animals and we need good association. We want to love and serve God. The problem is any social group in this world is full of half-truths, that's just the nature of groups, but the rarity of the thing does not preclude its existence, and we can only do the best we can.

And if the higher existence calls us to regretfully give up one level of association for a higher one, what can we do? Either bite the bullet so to speak and keep our mouth shut and live in our current society, or take the risk to give up the lower, not knowing where the higher will lead.

Even if it leads to perceived loneliness, that loneliness must be temporary as are all things in this world. To sacrifice the external manifestation of our high ideal for social peace, or to boldly go where few have gone before? That is the question, at least for me.

This book is a humble attempt to go where few have gone before, the evolutionary further line of God consciousness.

Whatever your name for God is, please be sincere in serving God and in being a plant-based, ahimsa, abolitionist vegan.

Serving God is primary. We all want to do something, do something higher, something for the higher interest.

Advertisers and media generally want to excite lower interest in us, self-indulgent interest. We are meant for the higher. The lower cannot satisfy us in the long run because the lower is temporary. Technological progress is preponderantly false progress.

There is a song, "Never Can Say Goodbye", one verse of the lyrics goes like this: "I keep thinking that my problems soon are all going to work out, but there's that same unhappy feeling there's that anguish there's that doubt."

That anguish and doubt could be the inside knowledge that our lives here are temporary. Only the higher world is lasting and can give us real peace and fulfillment.

Speaking of anguish and doubt, did you know that the major organic growers and most of the home gardeners that buy organic fertilizer at the nursery or hardware store, used cow blood and pig brains, etc as organic fertilizer.

I sent an email to the major organic grower in California and that means in the world. I posed as a slaughterhouse waste enthusiast and asked them if they use this great type of organic fertilizer.

They wrote back that they did. I have the emails saved and backed up.

Did you ever wonder why organic became widely accepted but anti-GMO has not. They won't even require simple labeling of GMO.

These two things, organic and anti-GMO should have gone hand in hand. The reason they didn't is because organic is the perfect match for the use of slaughterhouse waste that formerly went to waste, to now be monetized. And that's what happened.

Organic that does not use slaughterhouse waste is called vegan organic or simply veganic. There is a small movement in that direction and it is easy to grow your own vegetables etc. using only plant-based fertilizer.

The higher world is sweet and affectionate. The world we see externally with our material eyes is less than sweet and affectionate. Lower consciousness versus higher consciousness.

We need to constantly remind ourselves of the higher world and to associate with those that remind us of the peaceful promise of the higher world. The higher world exists but we have to be active in only serving that higher sweet world.

And now may God show you Supreme Beauty and Absolute Truth. Thank you very much.

Chapter 16
God Is Eternity, And We Are Property - God's Property

In this chapter we will discuss the factual sad fallen material situation we are all in, *but* which has such a high loving potential.

As we said in other chapters God is Eternity and we are property, God's property. We are being used by God in a loving way. We are God's property with the gift of an infinitesimal free will. Proper use of that free will is to surrender to God's purpose, and that purpose is inconceivably beautiful but we can't see it now.

Words have a difficult time describing things so deep but we are going to try, so please forgive our failings.

Pure love among humans (I can't speak for any other species other than saying that they too have the potential for affection, it cannot be denied), pure love among humans almost doesn't exist.

Your writer can only parrot what other few special souls have stated throughout human history and that is that God has given us free will to love God or to separate ourselves from God. Our small free will is the set-up for God's inconceivably beautiful purpose for us.

We are all daily killers in this world, so how does inconceivable beauty come from that? Maybe a story will help.

Imagine a little child is lost, separated from their parents in Grand Central Station in New York City. There could be a scarier place to be lost, like in Walmart, but for now it's Grand Central Station. Picture it, people are madly rushing here and there. The echoes of bustling noise is nerve-racking. Thousands of people roaming around and a few unscrupulous persons are among them no doubt.

In a situation like that being lost, who is more terrified, the parents or the child? Now by some miracle the child remembers that their parents said that people in uniforms are generally here to help us. So the child goes to a policeman, a service man, a pastor, or a nurse and says please help me. I'm lost from my parents.

That's the first step of redemption, of being found. And after agonizingly long intervening steps, a sound comes over the loudspeaker, and then the reunion happens. Imagine what those feelings of reunion and relief are in both the parents and the child.

This is the reunion that God is waiting for. It's between God and you, the intermediaries play a role no doubt but the most intense feelings are individual and personal to the two parties. In the worldly example it's between the parents and the child, but in the Divine realm it's between God the Supreme Loving Person and the little lost baby soul.

Words alone cannot describe, but maybe a song will help:

Amazing grace how sweet the sound
That grace my fear relieved
And God who calls me here below will be forever mine.

And now may God find you and you find God. Thank you very much.

Chapter 17
What Are The Three Types Of Milk?

Now some people think that taking milk from factory farmed cows is OK because cows are not killed at the time of milking, ignoring the gross mistreatment and the very soon to come slaughter.

Others think that taking milk from cows that are well cared for and allowed to die of old age is OK, ignoring the ropes, chains, pens, fenced fields and gender manipulation.

The true ahimsa abolitionist plant-based, vegan, no-milk people, think it is not right to either kill or imprison any animals. Free animals not suffering from **Stockholm Syndrome** (see next paragraph) value their freedom as much as humans do.

Stockholm Syndrome is when a captive prisoner, as a self-defense mechanism, becomes mentally attached to and sympathetic with its captors. Look it up.

Now in a different vein, slightly different vein, but you will see where this is going shortly - chanting God's Holy Name is something that can be done anytime, anywhere, in happiness or distress. That is to say that chanting God's Holy Name is beyond time and place, happiness or distress.

From Bhagavad Gita it goes something like this: "Happiness and distress are like sunrise and sunset, or summer and winter, they can't be stopped by us. The sufferings of the cycle of birth and death and the surety of death leaves only devotion to God as the sane alternative to the insanity of trying to enjoy our temporary bodies or of trying to create material equality in this world."

Devotion to God is generally agreed-upon by all theistic persons but there are many disagreements about exactly who is God and what is God's personality, who God's representative is, and about living habits in pursuit of devotion to God.

One thing that is generally agreed-upon in spiritual circles, at least in the saintly section of spiritual persons, is the principle of ahimsa, doing no or the least harm to others. In other words, giving honor to others.

So what does it all mean? It means that we are meant to worship God, chant God's name by whatever name we know God, and follow a plant-based vegan diet because that is the *least* harm being done to others while maintaining our own existence. And if it is a healthy whole-food diet, the *least* harm to our own physical and mental body.

Plus, and this is very important, according to both Genesis 1.29, and Bhagavad Gita 9.26 exactly as it is, a vegan diet is the diet that pleases God and that God wants us to follow in the unfallen state. A leaf, a flower, fruit and water.

Struggling and suffering are the reactions to not pleasing God by not accepting God's offered mercy and instruction, including as it turns out much suffering is the reaction to not following God's specific dietary requests in the Scriptures.

The three types of milk are slaughter milk, imprisoned slave milk, and no milk.

And now may God show you Absolute Truth and Supreme Beauty. Thank you very much.

Chapter 18
Why Is God Free And Eternal?

First of all I want to thank so many people for liking the draft of the immediately preceding chapter titled, "What are the Three Types of Milk?"

Sometimes this world seems pretty absurd, and although this is not our home we are still forced to make some kind of home here at least temporarily. How absurd is that!

Now the question is, while here should we get lost in activity in helping others, or in worshiping God directly. Well the answer is yes, the activity of helping others to remember God is the most noble activity to get lost in.

Not to simply push one's traditional elaborately constructed conception, that is after all like the six blind men investigating the elephant, and touching the different parts, and getting different ideas of what the elephant is without having ever actually seen the whole elephant. But to remind people that this world is not our home, and that somehow, somewhere over the rainbow God is watching, waiting for us to look that way and to make it to the other side so to speak.

So please remember that this world is not our home. Always remember that at all times and in all places. And that God is there in our real home waiting for us.

Hope And Mercy

The words hope and mercy are the two words that pretty much describe our predicament. We are always away from home and we need God's mercy to get back home again.

We cannot stay in this world for more than about 100 years. How is it our home?

The funny thing is that all of us, so-called saint or sinner, all of us, need God's mercy. Yes, some are more saintly than others but as the old saying goes in Romans 3.23, all have sinned and fallen short of the glory of God.

All have sinned and we need to be saved or at least forgiven. Is there a way to guarantee God's mercy, God's forgiveness? Is God's mercy guaranteed? That's the question. Can anything we do force or guarantee that God will act in a certain way? The question is, is God free and unbound or not? Is God, God, or our servant?

We all need God's mercy due to our daily killing of at least plants. If we are saved one day and then the next day we sin by killing again, which we do every day by eating at least plants and even by breathing in airborne entities. Justify it all you want, but it remains killing. Are we still saved or do we have to be saved again, and again, and again every day, or heaven forbid, after every meal? After every bite?

How can we kill constantly without needing God's mercy at every second and every breath? And again God is free, unless God is free and unbound God is not God. That God is free and unbound, that's part of God's greatness.

I may be mortal but at least someone, namely God is free and eternal. That should be enough to make us happy; that is home, that is mercy.

I may not even exist but God is free and eternal. Oh happy day.

And now may God show us Absolute Truth and Supreme beauty. Thank you very much.

Chapter 19
Where East And West Agree

Both Genesis and the Bhagavad Gita describe a plant-based vegan diet for embodied humans. Why do we deviate, when did we deviate? Mostly at least 10,000 years ago with the domestication, which means the enslavement of animals. Prior to that, smaller groups of humans lived mostly in warm wet fruit abundant tropics. Only very rarely did humans eat small animals and freshly, already dead larger ones.

The intelligent religious class of India at least, decided not to eat the poor domesticated captive cows and other animals. We deviate because of selfishness, "I am the Lord" mentality. While we are exploiting and stealing from the poor animals, we block out what it is we are actually doing, because we are trying to enjoy.

The Internet has made gruesome videos available that once accidentally, or purposely viewed, shock many young, uninvested, compassionate persons into instantly becoming vegan. And the Internet also enables those same beautiful people to easily find other like-minded souls.

How can we feed someone else's children to our own children? When challenged we act as if we are the offended ones, we are the offended party.

It's time to return home back to where God wants us to be under God's protective instruction as per Bhagavad Gita 9.26 and Genesis 1.29, the point where East and West agree on a common cause.

Now, somewhere over the rainbow real love without killing to eat exists. How did Dorothy in the Wizard of Oz go home? How did she wake up from her illusion? That illusion would be this world of killing folks.

She was chanting, not exactly God's names, but was chanting what is God's abode, which is our home. "There's no place like home, there's no place like home, there's no place like home." So to get out of this place and never come back we can take our cue from Dorothy and her friends, thinking, feeling and willing; the Scarecrow, the Tin Man and the Lion respectively. Thinking, feeling, and willing.

Mercy, God's mercy took Dorothy home. But Dorothy had a part to play. What was that part? That part was her strong desire, pure desire to go home. Dorothy said, "All I kept saying to everybody was I want to go home, I want to go home."

That's the only thing Dorothy wanted above all else, and click, click, along with God's mercy, that did it. There is no place like h OM e.

And now may God show us the Absolute Truth and Supreme Beauty. Thank you very much.

Chapter 20
The Shocking Truth About Spiritual Ahimsa And Mundane Sustainability

Surrender means to not spring back, to tolerate, to weather the storm so to speak. At times it is very difficult to do so. If someone is physically attacking your mother right in front of you for example, are you going to tolerate that? Probably not.

But that type of tolerance is not what we are talking about here. What we are talking about are attacks upon our pre-preconceived mental images, our material ego identities. We are only here for a very short time, so any material ego identity is a bit illusory . And being actors on a stage, it is best to not be overly attached to our illusory conceptions.

Whatever we have gathered in the past in the way of real truth can't be taken away from us, and we may even learn something if we are silent and listen to a little criticism once in a while.

On a slightly different note, but related: there is goal, and there is process. Where we're going and how we're going there. The destination and the journey.

The goal of life is to surrender to the Holy Name of variegated God. The going way is via humility, tolerance, and giving honor to others, ahimsa.

God is force field yes, but more than that God is Personality, Supreme Personality. Force field is more or less homogeneous, and personality is definitely variegated.

God the Supreme Person is dynamic and variegated. As spirit souls we are coequal with all other created spirit souls. This idea reveals a philosophical difference between Eastern and Western religions and philosophy. Western theism postulates dominion. It is not a minor difference between coequal with created souls and dominion over them.

One conception leads to a harmonious attitude towards the environment, the other conception leads to the present dominant world culture. The modern move toward sustainability is bifurcated in foundational concept by these two quite different ideas. So when we hear someone speak of sustainability we should try to be aware of which philosophy the speaker is following, coequal or domination? The difference between the two is a bit hidden, and lots of confusing half-truths are bandied about, by both sides. In fact one side may on the surface look exactly like the other side.

The eastern coequal conception should more likely lead to a vegan outlook, while the western dominion conception should more likely lead to organic meat. So amid all political confusion, sustainability is not the thing, foundational conception is the thing.

Now, the coequal conception of spiritual souls is, in fact, subject to evolution of purity. What is meant by this is that for a very many centuries India was a champion and source of Ahimsa. The modern vegan movement has at least some of its roots in England, as the person who coined the word Vegan was from the UK. It is no coincidence that the UK is the western country with the strongest ties to India.

In hindsight, India crafted a mass culture that went as far as it could at the time, to implement a society based on ahimsa. Subconsciously - and here's a caveat, I could be right or I could be wrong about this, but India knew it was still exploiting cows, and so they went to great lengths to Deify cows to mask deeply hidden and deep rooted guilt for making an expedient exception to non-interference with coequal's.

On the surface though, they explained that the COW was given by God to them for their use, just like the Westerners say that ALL animals were given by God to them for their use. However, the ahimsa principle, based on the all created spirit souls are equal conception, is very deeply rooted in the Indian psych and one can see that the younger generation of city dweller Indians especially, when they catch the vegan conception, they catch it fully along with it all its vegan type sustainability ramifications.

Now all of this is a little bit mundane and the fact is this world is not our home, nor anyone's. So again the spiritual conception is the thing and not material sustainability.

All glory to eternal God and to all the devotees of eternal God. And now may God show us the Absolute Truth and Supreme beauty. Thank you very much.

Chapter 21
Pandemic Of Half-Truth, And God's Full Stunning Beauty

You may have heard the saying, "Half-truth is more dangerous than total falsehood", or the updated version, "Half-fake news is more dangerous than full fake news.

Now with a show of hands, how many of you have ever seen, or at least heard of an old U.S. TV detective show called Dragnet? If you have, go ahead and raise your hands, don't be shy, no one's going to see you. (Yeah I know I can't see you either, but right now I am imagining.) You may be familiar from seeing that show, or possibly from seeing the Perry Mason show or some more modern show, sorry I don't watch TV or crime movies or television programs anymore, you may be familiar but the main part of the oath or affirmation given before sworn testimony in a court of law is "The truth, the whole truth, and nothing but the truth." And specifically from Dragnet, "Just the facts ma'am, just the facts."

The idea in that oath is to limit half-truth, by in effect pointing out some methods of delivering half-truths which are: 1) Giving only part of the truth and 2) By adding untruths to the narrative.

The material world is a problem of half-truth. Enter Satan. Do you think that full truth will ever exist here in this material world, between the bookends of birth and death? If you do, I've got some nice swamp land for sale in Florida.

Following is another one of the techniques of confusing facts, whether coming from organized government propagandists or from wanna be group leaders, bogus gurus or internet influencers, and there are a virtually unlimited number of wordsmiths that spew out many half-truths. These subtle or gross propagandists most often use a technique whereby they initially give a whole lot of truth, and then when you are sufficiently invested in the narrative, you become disarmed to the inevitable included falsehoods.

Why are there virtually unlimited persons spouting half-truths? Well, because without half-truths no one has any claim to position or originality. And why is that? Because God is the only original truth, full truth, and nothing but the truth. God is the only full truth. Pretty much everything else in heaven and earth is half-truth.

In Bhagavad Gita Lord Krishna says to abandon all varieties of religion [and politics], and surrender directly and exclusively to God.

How do we protect ourselves from ubiquitous half-truths? By sincerely looking towards and searching for the whole truth knowing that most everyone is throwing half-truth towards us and that we have to be always alert to detect half-truth, and not to ignore, skip over, or turn a blind eye to even apparently small half-truths.

If something stinks or smells fishy don't ignore it. You may have to give up something to climb higher, but how much true courage and actual honor do we have? Dwelling in cautionary country, may be only preparatory to the nectar of actually receiving the whole truth, and that whole truth is that this world is a crazy place and is not, and never will be a place for anyone to ever want to live in. Because we are constant remorseless killers of at least plants, this place is the actual hell of all conceptions of hell.

In a gross mundane example from the world of song, a hint of the whole truth can be found in the song, "Pretty Woman", sung by Roy Orbison and co-written by Roy Orbison. The words I'm referring to are: "Pretty woman, I don't believe you, you're not the truth." The full Absolute Truth is God the Supreme Beautiful Person, as mirrored in a beautiful sunset, a majestic towering mountain, the stars at night in the still dark desert sky, and the sound of steady rain on a tin roof while sheltering in a secluded forest cabin. If God is only one thing, God is stunningly beautiful.

I think we have all gotten at least a little glimpse of God's Supreme Beauty, otherwise how could we survive existing in this horrible world of constant unending killing and quarreling. God is everything. God is our destination. God is our home. Don't we all love home?.

And now may Sweet God show us the Truth, the Whole Truth, and Nothing But the Truth. Thank you very much.

Chapter 22
What Is The Passage Back To God And What Is The Arrival?

Now, God is our source. And God is our destiny. We may spiritualize our lives by always remembering, and never forgetting God. Remember God in the morning. Never forget God during the day. And always remember God, in the evening. You can even dream of God at night.

The easiest way to serve and remember God is to feed God. It's simple because we eat all the time, generally three times every day. And it's simple because God tells us what to eat and what to offer God. In Bhagavad Gita 9.26 - a leaf, a flower, fruit and water, and in Genesis 1.29 - every seed-bearing plant on the face of the earth and every tree that has fruit with seed in it.

Just see how loving God is. No slaughterhouses, or slaughterhouse waste used as organic fertilizer in heaven. Heaven is a stage of consciousness that takes some seriousness. Heaven is real, beyond time & space - and beyond even thought. You can't think your way into heaven. Only by God's mercy and your surrender to God.

One aspect of God is that, as the one-and-only SUPREME ENJOYER, God is the playful, sweetest, rascal sense enjoyer of everything, but God is also inconceivably, simultaneously, the GRIEF-STRICKEN OBSERVER of the pained pastimes, of the minutely-free embodied souls in this world (that's us by the way).

In any case, God is the OBSERVER of the embodied soul's dramatic struggles to break free of constant forgetfulness of God's infinite beauty - which forgetfulness is what is going on while we are within this killing field of eating others, during the infinitesimal time between birth and death, ironically called "life".

Ironic also, is the fact that, THIS MATERIAL WORLD is - to use the musical group the Eagles phrase - "the PASSAGE back, to the PLACE I was before", and that transcendental place is also indicated in ISKCON's Shrila Prabhupada's phrase, "Back home, back to Godhead."

And "death", what then is death? Death is the ARRIVAL back home - this world is the passage - death is the ARRIVAL back home, back to the ONLY place of peace, with no killing, and no tears. As singer Eric Clapton has sung, "Beyond the door there's peace I'm sure, and I know, there'll be no more tears, in heaven."

And now may God show us Absolute Truth and Supreme Beauty. Namaste, amen, and muchas gracias.

Chapter 23
How Do We Find Deep Peace Within Ourselves And Only Think Of God's Happiness?

Hi, I'm an aspiring servant of God.

All want peace. But all do not know how to get it. Surrender to dominance, ultimately to God's dominance is the formula for peace. We will get back to this idea in a moment, but first and related to surrender, is tolerance:

When things are going well, tolerance is fairly easy to do. But when periodic disasters occur, or when obstacles appear, that's when tolerance becomes a little more difficult.

Tolerance is a facet of sense control. And of the senses the mind is the center. But even when we have made a DECISION to control the mind and senses in a particular way, it is DIFFICULT to control the Mind.

Even if we APPROACH perfect sense control, still because we are killing and eating vegetables everyday, or at the very least we are killing tiny microbes in the air when we breathe, so as constant killers, we always need God's mercy, especially at the time of death.

We must tolerate everything, and pray that God can tolerate us, our daily killing.

God's merciful tolerance is everything to us. We want tolerance from God, so we should give tolerance to others as much as possible.

Now as was said at the beginning, all want peace. But all do not know how to get it. Surrender to dominance, ultimately to God's dominance, is the formula for peace. Surrender and tolerance are similar things.

God's dominance is time, the march of time, which is death. Time deals with everyone. Essentially we do not have to take action about any kind of Justice. Time takes care of that.

Now, most people are keenly aware of, and concerned with their own and their family's immediate future, and eternal future.

Preachers throughout history have been SELLING the guarantee of a personal eternity.

"Just believe, and you will have eternity." This may be true. Nonetheless, it is a little self-centered.

Because if God is your ONLY HERO, and God is honestly your Only True Beloved, then you would *ONLY* think of God's happiness, and not of your own.

God is eternal and God is Supremely Beautiful - of this there is no doubt. Regardless of what happens to us, *that* is, or should be enough for "Peace in the Valley".

Your future is in God's hands not your own.

It's not, "I don't want to die." or even "I do want to die." It's only, "I love you, God."

No thought of your own future, only of God's happiness, equals peace in the Valley.

From the song, "Peace In The Valley", by Thomas A. Dorsey:

"Well the bear, will be gentle, and the wolves, will be tame
And the lions shall lay down by the lamb, oh yes

And the beasts, from the wild, will be led, by a child
And I'll be changed, changed from this Creature that I am, oh yeah

There will be peace in the valley, someday
There will be peace in the valley, oh Lord, I pray

There'll be no sadness, no sorrow, no trouble, trouble I see
There will be peace in the valley for me, for me."

And now may God show us the Absolute Truth and Supreme Beauty.

Namaste, amen and muchas gracias.

Chapter 24
Divine Love Requires Freedom

Doesn't matter what happened in the past, this is now, leave the cows alone.

It's not simply about eating or not eating meat, it's about killing and exploiting those you have power over. Unnecessarily exploiting those you have power over is the definition of being a bad person.

Yes, Dorothy, vegans are also killing plants. So even vegans need God's mercy at the time of death.

However, there is a common-sense difference between eating plants and eating animals, and if you *can't* see that in the following example may God have mercy on you:

Take your innocent beautiful child to a park for a picnic on a sunny Sunday afternoon, where many other families with children are happily running and frolicking about. Lay down your clean blanket on the soft green grass near the idyllic pond filled with gentle swimming swans, while other birds sing sweetly in the trees, and you are cooled by a gentle summer breeze. Now partake of your picnic fair of sweet and juicy fresh fruits, like mangos and strawberries, and lightly cooked and pleasingly spiced vegetable preparations. How beautiful and happy a scene.

Take it in - breathe in the fresh air.

Now take your child to a slaughterhouse for a picnic.

Want me to describe that for you?

There's a difference. Please see that, and immediately become a committed total plant-based diet eater. Vegetarian is not good enough. The cows are being held prisoner, even at temples in India, and are gender exploited and manipulated. And as was previously stated, exploiting innocent entities that one has power over is the definition of being a creep, a low life, a despicable dictator, a punk, a demon, or at best a soul not yet able to accept. Do we get the idea yet to stop unnecessarily exploiting cows?

Doesn't matter what happened in the past, it matters what is happening now. The ingredient in cow's milk that was necessary for healthy brain and nerve function, namely vitamin B12 is well known and easily available now from non-animal sources. Therefore, keeping cows even only as prisoners with ropes around their neck, kept in sheds or imprisoned in fenced fields, not to speak of their sexual exploitation, is now clearly unnecessary exploitation. Doesn't matter what happened in the past, this is now, leave the cows alone.

If our knowledge and hardware change, we adapt and change with that changing knowledge. Does anyone use an old style typewriter or Ma Bell crank telephone any more? So why keep cows unnecessarily captive to get necessary for fine brain and nerve function Vitamin B12 when B12 is now easily available from non-animal sources because it comes from bacteria in the soil. Complete the ahimsa principle of giving honor to others, and non-exploitation of the poor *Stockholm Syndrome* suffering cows. Adapt to change, grow up and be a noble person.

We will end with a quote from one Jason Versey:

"Even a spineless arthropod sheds what's no longer useful and leaves it behind them. Are you not more intelligent than they?"

And now may God show us Absolute Truth and Supreme Beauty. Thank you very much.

Chapter 25
The Meaning Of Divine Love

Except for God's presence in the world, Pure Love only exists on the other sides of birth and death.

The thing that goes by the word "LOVE" in the material world - due to daily constant killing to eat, and just by breathing - so-called "love" in the material world is simply individual and group selfishness. Daily killing to eat is the infinite elephant in the room that everyone completely ignores or makes prayers about to appease and "thank" God, as if it's God's idea that we are in this Fallen State, without fault of our own. Fallen State because we are in hell right now, it's not a fictional future. Hell is here, now. Unless you're a slick marketer, then this is Paradise."

The so-called **circle of life** could just as equally be called the circle of life *and* death.

The so-called "life" part sustains itself via eating, in other words, on the death and dismemberment, or at least the disturbance and selfish taking advantage of one by another. So, really, the material world is MOST accurately called the cycle or circle of unending death. Bad. But don't worry because this chapter will end with what is "good".

Now exactly why is unending death and the eating of others bad? Duh. Because we wouldn't want it done to us, you know like being eaten by the Kanamits in the Twilight Zone season 3, episode 24.

A human life of **renunciation** is always **incomplete**, including if one only eats fruits and leaves that fall from trees, because when you walk over to the tree, you are stepping on and killing small insects. Even when one is FASTING until death, behold, floating single-celled entities that you breathe in are being disturbed and killed. As the Christians and others say, we can't earn our way into God's presence. Constant killing & exploitation of others is why. God is the only one with the RIGHT to kill and exploit. And if you don't like THAT, who ya gonna call?

The thing called "life" is problematic at best. And again, it is not actually a nice thing, despite all the beautiful sunsets and smiling babies.

Except if one comes back to material embodiment, the saying, "They went to a better place." is probably true. Hell is the place of death and destruction, and death and destruction *is* what's going on *right here, right now* in this embodied life. This is actual fact.

"We gotta get out of this place, if it's the last thing we ever do." is a great sentiment.

Divine Love manifested as Mercy at the time of death, is the closest real love gets to the material embodiment. A slight correction is an order, actually, in a way our birth into this material **hell** is also God's **mercy** and real love. Why is that? Because without us having the free will and choice to come here - and we had that free choice - there is no meaning to Divine love. Divine love is a free transaction between God and the individual infinitesimal free living beings when they realize they made the wrong choice to forget about God. Except for **God's** personal presence in the material world, pure love is not to be found among embodied entities between birth and death, only on the other side.

The way to get out of this hellish place of remorseless enjoyment of constant killing to eat, and to never come back, is by complete, unending devotion to God, while simultaneously acknowledging our utter despicableness. Go from remorseless enjoyment of constant killing - to remorseful of our complicitness, constant remembrance of our loving, and oh so tolerant God. God is Good.

And now may God show us Absolute Truth and Supreme Beauty.

Thank you very much.

Chapter 26
What Does Abolitionist Vegan Mean?

Just like in the middle of the 19th century in the U.S., the word "abolition" meant freedom for the slaves, today Abolitionist Vegan means Freedom for the animals, In other words for animals NOT to be slaves of humans.

It's a pretty simple idea, no person should be the "owned" property of another person. Similarly no animal should be the property of any other animal. And duh humans are a type of animal.

Animals eat, humans eat; animals sleep, humans sleep; animals mate, humans mate; animals fight, and humans drop atomic bombs. Who is better? So why can a human not own another person, but can own an animal? Because a human can create and drop an atomic bomb? It's crazy.

Now here I must give a warning of unpleasant graphic language to come. Please forgive me, it's just coming out and I am not censoring it. There's too much censorship today. The following is somewhat harsh and to the point so if you don't like that kind of thing, please forgive me and skip over reading the next one paragraph.

Here is more craziness - treat a dog or a cat like a family member or even like a king, or a queen, and simultaneously treat other, mostly peaceful grazing animals, like trash or even less than trash - cut off their beaks, grind up their bones, and dry and powder their blood to become certified organic fertilizer. Or make hamburger out of old dairy cows whose milk and cheese you buy for your festivals. Or keep "protected" cows as life-long prisoners, gender abused cows suffering from very real *Stockholm Syndrome*. Look it up if you haven't already done so.

Material and technical evolution is false evolution. Real Evolution is Evolution of Consciousness - like in abolishing human slavery, and now like abolishing animal slavery, which animal slavery is euphemistically, and falsely called "animal agriculture".

It's not animal AGRI-culture - it's animal slave culture, or animal slaughter culture.

Here next is another one paragraph to skip reading if you don't like graphic description.

So the next time you cuddle your cat or pet your dog, listen for the screams of the other poor docile grazing animals as the finely honed, sharp, cold-steel edge of the guillotine blade slams down on their necks, and the blood squirts out of their severed arteries until there is no fight left in them. Sad.

Humans think they are so great, and that is the real problem of this world. Humans think, "Well I can build a skyscraper and land my booster rocket back on the surface of the earth to be reused, so therefore I must be great. I can do anything." Yeah? Well then eliminate death - today, not in some fairytale future.

God can continue your life today, or stop your life today, And God could always do that in the past and will always be able to do that in the future. Who are we!? Punks, creeps, low-life's. Our bombs only destroy and our rockets only send diseases and deadly viruses throughout the universe.

Stop thinking we're so great as being a member of the human species. The human species has the potential for real greatness, yes, but that real greatness is not what we normally think of as greatness. Human potential greatness, is to really see how we are constant killers and enslavers of others - plant species or animal species. And to really see that we don't like it when we are called out as constant killers. We can't stop killing until God makes the final call and we get out of this place. Really. Thank God that that is the last thing we'll ever do in this world of death. To get out of it.

Sorry for the rant. No more negatives, only positives. God is beautiful, inconceivably Beautiful. And God is loving, inconceivably loving. How does God tolerate us as individual humans or as the species of humans?

Do we owe anything to God? Of course we do. We owe everything to God. Everything! God is our father, God is our mother, God is our friend, God is our mentor. God is creator, God is destroyer. God is judge, jury, prosecutor and police. But because God, who is all things, is also our lover, and our beloved, God sleeps dreaming of us. But inconceivably and simultaneously God couldn't care less about us. Just see God's majesty and greatness.

We have no sane choice but to reciprocate love with God. How do we do that? Think about God, speak about God, write about God. Everything about God. Make movies about God. But what do we know about God? We are like little children who can't speak, and can't even remember the day when we learned to stand up on our own two feet.

Memory? What will be our last memory? Will we remember God? Will we remember that we are not God and that only

God has the right to do anything. Anything. That *we* have no right to kill animals or even to kill plants. But remember there is a gradation between killing plants and killing and eating animal products - and that's the difference between taking a child to a beautiful park for a picnic of sweet fruits, and taking a child to a slaughterhouse for a picnic.

We are less than nothing, less than the dust in the wind. We are not even zero, we are negative. God is the only sweet positive. God is the Greatest and Most Beautiful. Hallelujah and a slave-free, cow-free Hare Krishna.

And now may God show us all, Absolute Truth and Supreme Beauty.

Thank you very much.

Chapter 27
If I Had The Wings Of An Angel

What does God want from us? God wants us to come to God. To give up all varieties of religion and religious organizations, and to give up all varieties of politics and current events, forget all that and focus everything you've got - focus everything on God. What else can we do, that's what God wants. Because this is the land of killing, God wants us out of here.

Why am I engaging in material-world related temporary causes that can not have a solution?

To focus everything on God is the highest conception - what's the highest conception? To focus everything on God. This is called devotion to God - or in one Sanskrit word: Bhakti. Bhagavan Bhakti is the most radical thing one can do in their whole life, that is the sum total goal of life, and to put it most simply that is what God wants from us - to focus everything on God. That is the purpose of everything. To extremely, radically give up everything else and to come directly, and utterly and completely to God.

What should one do with one's time. To do service for others, also called working for the benefit of others, is considered a high calling. To serve or work for God is the highest calling. Is all service, service to God? Well that depends on who benefits from the service, or who the work is directed to.

The scientists did a lot of hard work and scientific type service developing an atomic bomb, right? Well that maybe wasn't exactly the best service to God. By dropping an atomic bomb on 100,000+ people, that wasn't maybe a pure service to God.

But LOVING service, done directly to God - that's a horse of a different color, that is fairly easy to identify. Chanting

God's name, singing and speaking and writing God's glories. It is a very simple thing, to serve God. We just have to make that decision, that choice. It's a free choice. That's what God wants, our free choice to serve God in a favorable, simple way.

Deal with the world in a minimum way, only as required, but not too much. Be simple & be non-envious.

Now because one of our main activities in this fallen life is eating, we can specifically, easily spiritualize our daily living by preparing food to be offered to God, as per God's literal vegan request in Holy Scripture Bhagavad Gita 9.26 & Genesis 1.29, and then we take that offered and spiritualized food for our sustenance.

We generally have to work or do some gainful employment for a living. The best we can do there, is to offer the fruits of those endeavors to the Lord. And the regular daily activities of reading about God, singing about God, thinking about God, and so forth, keep us on track to always remember God and never forget God. [Sing if you know the tune] "God in the morning, God in the evening, God at suppertime; God is sweeter than sugar, let's love God, all the time." Maybe that was a little frivolous, but you get the idea - God is everything, and we should do everything for God.

[Sing] "Oh if I had the wings of an Angel, over these prison walls I would fly, and I'd fly to the arms of my sweet Lord, and there I'd be willing to die." Adapted from "The Prison Song".

And now may God show us Absolute Truth and Supreme Beauty. Thank you very much.

Chapter 28
Lovingly Calling Out To God

Even if we could move to another planet with a younger sun than ours, that sun would eventually burn out and explode.

So, this world is doomed one way or the other. What to speak of this world, our physical bodies are doomed to live to only a maximum of approximately 100 years.

Limited time offers (that's this material world folks) are psychologically compelling only if we are foolish shallow thinkers. All offers of this world are limited time offers, including "sustainability." Don't be foolish to fall for all the hype about anything that is touted as so important. The nearby sun will explode, as will every star, one after another.

The world is dead, why beat a dead horse?

Let's look at the "great" call of sustainability which is nice but ultimately is also doomed along with every other temporary cause. To engage in this cause more than just in passing is a waste of our valuable LIMITED TIME. This does not mean we should not be sustainable in our personal living - we should be - but there is another much more important topic, namely God.

This is a really big point that pretty much divides eternal theistic thinking, from being fooled by a temporary desire that seems so important. There are many, many arguments why sustainability is sooooo important, and that if you don't give your life to this cause "you are not a good person, you are evil, you don't support the atheistic UN organization's Agenda 21 and its update the 2030 Agenda for Sustainable Development." Secular means atheistic.

Again there is nothing wrong with personal sustainable living, but an atheistically run global totalitarian, authoritarian government run by so-called elite technocrats with 1984 type surveillance systems, is not the way.

It is self-evident that God is the cause of all causes. Trying to love God by loving ANY temporary cause in this temporary world, will get you just that - temporary results. Temporary results that are gone with the wind.

Don't.

Aren't you tired of temporary? "All things must Pass" is the material world. God does not "pass". So intelligence tells us to go for the only absolutely permanent thing i.e. - God.

A little kid can understand this. But we can't because we are corrupted with the attachment to "independent desire", local interest if you will, temporary interest. Unrestricted sense gratification.

The relativists say, "Why not unrestricted sense gratification?" The atheistic relativists also say, "There's no God, there's no one we are responsible to. Make all the babies you want, just be sure you kill them before they are born." And some of these demons even want you to kill your baby shortly after it's born.

God is hidden behind a curtain, like the way the Wizard of Oz was hidden behind a curtain.

This does not mean God cannot reveal God's self, or that God won't let Toto pull back the curtain. But generally God is unknown and unknowable, at least a lot of the time. Does God like to play hide and seek? That little rascal.

God, however, has revealed Genesis 1.29 and Bhagavad Gita 9.26 wherein, although God can be whatever God wants to be, God has that right, you know, God asks us to be loving vegans: "I give you every seed-bearing plant and every tree that has fruit." Genesis 1.29. And "Offer me with love and devotion, a leaf, a flower, fruit and water." Bhagavad Gita 9.26. Many Buddhists are also tending towards plant-based vegan.

Whether via scripture or by observation, one can see that mass culture is going down morally. Watch TV & movies from the 1950's versus what you see now.

"Liberation from past stifling morality" is mostly Newspeak or marketing speak for the degradation of what is high and virtuous.

The good news is that for whatever reason more and more enlightened souls are beginning to follow what has been recommended in Holy Scripture for a long, long time, and that is the vegan diet as mentioned in Bhagavad Gita 9.26 and Genesis 1.29. Because of the importance of the activity of eating, without being plant-based vegan practically no one is following God's desire for us.

The material world is always the push-pull between good and bad. One side lifts us up in one way, and the other side drags us down in its way.

God in God's glory has given us a choice. Run after the temporary of this world, or go after the Absolute, who is God. In other words, to run after God's temporary created world of sense gratification, or to love God directly. Like what was said concerning "sustainability", loving God's created world yields temporary results at best. To love God directly is the only possibility for PERMANENT satisfaction. And if we are not following God's no animal-killing request for us, how can we hope to be loving and serving God directly?

Having established love for eternal God, beyond love for the temporary, as the goal of "life", what is the SURE way to serve, and thereby develop love for God?

One way is to follow God's instruction to be loving plant-based vegans in one's daily diet and habits.

But the biggest way to love God is to call out God's name. ANY bona fide name for God, but one of the best, if not *the* best name of God is Krishna. Why Krishna? Because Lord Shri Krishna clearly and directly asks us to be loving plant-based vegans in Bhagavad Gita 9.26 by requesting God be offered a leaf, a flower which could be the bud of the flower like broccoli and cauliflower etc., fruit and water.

God, like any loving parent or guardian would, wants us to lovingly call out one of God's many Holy Names. And according to God's request in both Holy scriptures Genesis 1.29 and Bhagavad Gita 9.26, God wants us most definitely to be loving plant-based vegans.

Find and associate with some good strict vegan-only, sense gratification restricted servants of God. There aren't many, but more are coming. Minimize association with hard-core vegetarian "cow protectors" with their ignorant twisted logic about how it is good to keep cows as chattel slavery property, because God "likes" cows and because the cows are "loved" by the "Devotees". Remember the captive cows are suffering from *Stockholm Syndrome*, whereby it is only on the surface that it appears that cows accept their imprisoned, gender exploited slavery.

At the present time it is not necessary to enslaved cows and steal their baby's milk to get vitamin B12 "for fine brain tissues", which necessary vitamin B12 can now be gotten from non-animal exploitive sources. As a vegetarian, to take milk in the past may have been all right, but not now, and this cannot be emphasized enough, it is not now at the present time alright for anyone, and anyone means anyone, to own and enslave gender manipulated cows. If one now owns a captive cow don't breed them or buy any more.

Life is killing, daily killing of either plants or animals. How can we expect "eternal life" after death if we are daily killing?

So this "life is sacred" B.S. statement is just that. Humans are killing other beings every day. This thing called material life is a bad thing. But we wish everyone a long life as the chance to realize how corrupt so-called "sacred life" actually is.

God's Holy Life is the only truly sacred life there is. We may be parts and parcels of God that's true, but the material world is definitely not a place for a gentle person.

Serve God by remembering, speaking, chanting and singing one of God's many Holy Names. Always remember to serve God and never forget to serve God, that is our home. The easy, happy way to humbly serve God is to chant or sing any one of God's Holy Names. And behave yourself by controlling your senses.

It is the most serious, but at the same time happy thing, to serve God.

Chant or sing God's Holy Name and be vegan, and don't let anyone try to tell you that being vegan is an optional thing, and is just only your personal choice. No! God specifically asks us to be vegan. No slaughter milk and no slave milk.

May God show us the truth, the whole truth, and nothing but the truth.

Thank you very much.

Chapter 29
Hidden Power Vs Innocent Surrender

Power in this world, versus surrender. There's the choice. The pitiable illusory sucker position of social dominance & technical and/or scriptural elitism, versus simple, sweet, helpful, motiveless, self-giving service.

A hang-up to the simple sweet, helpful, self-giving, motiveless service position, is the deep rooted desire to maintain one's hard earned dominant social and financial position of privilege. In other words would you give up your comfortable life, with an esteemed position in society, your hard earned comfortable life to publicly proclaim an unpopular major position that was not accepted in the past, nor connected to all the past funding traditions, but which major position is now clearly seen and can be shown to be an advancement of Godly surrender by those who have been blessed by that vision from God.

Consider yourself very blessed if God has given you the ability to see the clear difference between a totally, self-surrendered, fully truthful life without any self-serving compromises vs a dominant societal power position maintained by twisted, shameless, brain-washed, and mentally and physically hidden exploitation of a class of others, facilitated by kowtowing to one's complicit money sources, and to one's complicit hierarchical stone-like organizations.

There is only one gift greater from God than clearly seeing the shameless power vs uncompromised truth dichotomy, and that one greatest gift is the Freedom to decide which one of these two kinds of persons we want to be.

So, these are the two greatest gifts from God, freedom to choose and the vision to see what to choose to please God. Without these two things there is nothing for us.

Not you, not me, but us.

And now may God show you the Absolute Truth and Supreme Self-giving Loving Beauty.

Peace in fearless service to God.

Thank you very much.

Chapter 30
How To Fall Into God's Loving Arms

God is the Absolute Truth, and while God is free to do anything and everything God wants to do, by *various metrics* - God does *in fact* want us to follow a loving vegan diet, as stated respectively in Genesis 1.29 and Bhagavad Gita 9.2, "I give you all the plants with seeds and all trees with fruits" and "Offer God with love a leaf, a flower, fruit, and water." And as per the preponderance of modern plant-based scientific evidence the same is true.

God is the Source and the End of everything. God is Perfect Love and Perfect Beauty. Do you think Perfect Love and Perfect Beauty kills innocent animals or in the case of material cows, that perfectly loving and perfectly beautiful God wants us to keep innocent animals as Stockholm Syndrome suffering captive gender-exploited female, milk slaves?

Stockholm Syndrome is when, as a DEFENSE mechanism, prisoners become supportive of, sympathetic to, and apparently even affectionate with their captors. All these feelings go away in due course of time when the captives are rescued and restored to their natural free state.

Escaped or freed cows, bovines owned by Hawaiian Royalty very quickly returned to their natural free and open roaming condition on the Big Island of Hawaii. They hide on the forested slopes of the volcanos and will run away or fight you when you approach them. There are many online internet articles about free roaming Hawaiian cows and bulls, but be warned they are mostly written from a meat eaters perspective.

Turning to a slightly different but related subject:

Politically in the material world there is left and right. Without getting dragged down into that world, the point being made here is that we should take only the good from both sides without feeling any party spirit or joining any party. "Good" being defined as actions without negative reaction.

The "good" from the conservative right is the self-supportive work ethic - along with traditional-marriage, non-abortive morality, with acceptance of gender outliers but without over-emphatic glorification; and the "good" from the liberal left side of the isle is the tendency to give respect for all animals, manifest as a vegan diet.

And a third and final related subject:

How to fall into God's loving arms?

We superficially think death is the problem, but only death is the actual solution. God's eternal embrace.

Our deepest inner heart's fulfillment is not to be found within this world of constant killing and disturbance of others.

What we want, what we need, is a relationship with God. And we can't have the highest, deepest factual relationship with God if we disregard God's request of us in both Bhagavad Gita 9.26 and Genesis 1.29 to lovingly follow a plant-based vegan diet. In the past maybe, but now at the present time a lacto- so-called vegetarian diet is not enough.

Constant repetition of God's Holy Name as a memory aid, and to please God, is the recommended method to always remember God and never forget God. And because God is totally Free and Unbound, and can change things in an instant, God's Holy name is the only sure thing in eternity.

If you are head over heels in love with someone you are always thinking of them and speaking their name. In today's Godless civilization constant repetition of God's Holy name is the lifesaving activity and can be done anytime, anyplace.

In the most humble position one thinks that all restrictions and all requirements are for one's self, and that all others are pure and free. So there is no force, only voluntary action.

And now may God show you Absolute Truth and Supreme Beauty.

Thank you very much.

Chapter 31
Take The Good From The Left - And The Right

Generally - conservatives have morality, and respect for God on their side, while liberals have compassion for animals.

The Joker, Joaquin Phoenix from leftist Hollywood, gave the quintessential explanation of the philosophical basis for compassion for animals in his acceptance speech for his movie Oscar.

Conservatives mock leftist vegans as "soy boys" jumping on a false criticism implying that vegans are wimps and only animal killers are heroic. Among the ranks of vegans are tennis's Williams sisters, Sarina and Venus; Carl Lewis, winner of 9 Olympic gold medals for world's fastest runner; and world's strongest man Patrik Baboumian, winner of 18 Strongman and log lifting titles. Even ancient Roman gladiators were mostly animal-free, plant-based eaters.

Although most of these athletes are vegan for health and strength reasons, the immediate point here is that animal-eating conservatives falsely mock and belittle vegans. Big demerit for conservatives.

Now for the left's generally true demerit: Many leftists are godless "science answers ALL-questions" believers, with little if any respect for transcendental, traditional truth and beauty. Or maybe they give lip service to God to fool the gullible.

Science as the basis of a one size fits all mentality known by the term modernism, leads to a socialist, communist, "god-of-equality" bent. The far leftist philosophy is of oneness and equality. In other words all cultures are equal, and individually we are all EQUAL TO GOD.

That is the argument of the devil in the Garden of Eden, and is the gist of the thinking of some mayavad type Indians from India who now are CEO heads of and thereby control most of the biggest US originated tech companies - Alphabet, parent company of Google, and Youtube, Microsoft, IBM, Adobe, Twitter (fired November 2022) and an Indian was an early top executive of Facebook. Mayavad oneness-and-equality type Indians have assumed the leadership of many of the biggest tech companies and because many of them follow the hidden godless philosophy of oneness and equality, many do not hesitate to censor conservative views that don't fit the far leftist narrative.

Many of today's godless Indian oneness and equality mayavad (a person who believes all are one with and equal to God, therefore we are God and only have to answer to ourselves) run US tech companies are natural brothers of the godless CCP, the Chinese Communist Party. And if you work for one of those tech companies you are complicit, just like if you don't actually rob a bank but you willingly drive the getaway car.

The God of the philosophy of oneness and equality - is power. Truth is a non-consideration. Power, as an equal-of-God, is their sincerely held belief. Inside themselves, the far leftists think there is nothing wrong with untruth that serves the goal of power. Rarely can you convince them - not rarely, almost never can you convince a leftist that the power conception of existence (as opposed to the transcendental conception) is wrong, because they don't believe in right and wrong, they only believe in power, that's a fact. Get over it.

Now by God's arrangement the religious people do not need to defeat the factually atheist scientific equality and oneness mayavad philosophy. Religious people just need to wait things out and idle in place for a while so to speak. "Ye shall know the truth and the truth will set you free."

Here's the truth that's happening that will defeat the scientific rationalists without a fight:

The globalist, one size-fits-all scientists and technicians, in the spirit of the UN Agenda 21 and it's follow up the 2030 Agenda for Sustainability have decided for themselves to stop having babies via termination of the unborn, and via feminism whereby women become men. (Or men become women swimmers.)

And the religious people, rightly or wrongly not fearing sustainability doom, are continuing to have traditional larger families.

By God's ironic arrangement, godless people are self-exterminating. Now, just imagine and think about that for a moment.

Even more ironic is that actually it is the religious people that should be self-exterminating by restricting their mode-of-passion sense enjoyment. Because, if religious persons, who openly state that this world is not our home, and that we belong together with God in the spiritual world forever, if they truly believed that way they would remain celibate or do like Lord Jesus asked them to do, and would follow him, and would refrain from expanding the population of this fallen plane.

The good thing to be taken from the left is respect for the animals, not to eat them or steal their milk, which milk is not necessary for strength and health nor for brain function as we now have easily available vitamin B12 from non-animal exploitive sources.

The good things to be taken from the traditional right are, 1) belief in God, and 2) traditional morality, which has stood the test of time, since the beginning of time. Spiritually motivated morality, tends to evolve upward over time. Faster in some places than others, but the tendency is to evolve upward.

But wait, there's MORE to the idea of mor-ality. For every-day non-reactive action in this world, traditional morality is a good thing. But in the deepest sense, morality in this world is merely agreed-upon rules for exploitation of God's property. We have to give up the idea that in ANY way this material world is a good place, except for the one caveat, that the one good thing about this world, is that it is a place to REALIZE it is no good.

This material world is so full of faults, such that if the material world is the only thing we look to, we necessarily end up demoralized overtime. We MUST at least look towards God. That is the only sane position. God IS great. In Bhagavad Gita 18.66 God says to abandon all varieties of religion and politics and morality, and surrender directly, and exclusively, and personally to God.

Without joining any political party, take only the good from both sides - the left's non-interference with animals, and on the right side, traditional morality. But above all else always remember God, and never forget God.

And now may God show us the truth, the whole truth, and nothing but the truth.

Chapter 32
Real Religion Means Proper Adjustment

Karma, also known as action-and-reaction is a fact, in both physics and behavior. It is easier to climb onto a roof using a ladder, when we are on a higher rung than a lower rung. In the same way it is easier to reach heaven so to speak when we are on a higher moral rung, i.e., from a higher mode of material nature – namely the material mode of goodness.

Now, what are generally called moral principles, the 4 main ones being restriction from intoxication, gambling, animal product eating, and to be properly married, are in fact <u>time-tested principles of living a life FREE from karmic reactive TURMOIL.</u> It is simple behavioral physics. Breaking restrictions may temporarily feel good, but will get you sooner or later. Like the lyrics in the U.S. band the Eagles song Desperado: "…but these things that are pleasing you [apparently] can hurt you somehow." It is just good intelligence.

Related to wrong things that hurt you, the same God in both Genesis 1.29 and Bhagavad Gita 9.26 asks us to be loving vegans. Look it up.

So don't think of a *noble life* as being restrictive - except as *restrictive of turmoil in our lives*. Think of restriction of **reactive activity** as how to actually get that - "peaceful, easy feeling." You've got to WANT it.

Now, in the interest of Divine Harmony, "The only way" that Lord Jesus referred to is the "Transcendental Way". Not that God can't have more than one son, but that the Transcendental Way *is* the only way. And it's true.

And that Transcendental Way of life is the "*Love for the Holy Name for God way.*"

Not simply all the rituals and stories of the spiritual heroes of one's own particular spiritual tradition, that's fine, but mainly always being conscious of and serving the interest of the Holy Name for God, starting with the simple word "God" and including all the names meant for identifying the loving, merciful, free and unbound ahimsa Personality of God from all traditions; or even one's own name for God (all things are possible with God), so long as it is for the one loving and All-attractive, scriptural plant-based vegan requesting, and other non-reactive behavior requesting, Creator and Maintainer God.

God in Genesis and God, Krishna in Bhagavad Gita are the same one loving God. And according to Scripture, God requires of us, in a pure un-fallen existence, that we give full respect to animals by following God's, and now science's requested whole plant food pure diet. The Garden of Eden and the Promised Land are both vegan.

Please accept the peaceful life of not eating any animal products including taking milk from *Stockholm Syndrome* suffering captive and gender manipulated cow's, not taking intoxicants, not gambling and of properly married life.

And above all else, because God is Free & Unbound; and therefore, as the Holy Name for God is the only sure thing in eternity - please develop your innate love for God by sincerely and always chanting, singing, remembering, promoting and serving a Holy Name of Our Sweet Lord.

To become a leader in this current evolution of loving consciousness, only requires whole-hearted acceptance of a totally animal ahimsa-abolitionist view of God Consciousness, and to systemically adjust *that* throughout the rest of the historical spiritual philosophy and Scripture. An apparent *major* change maybe, but this **animal-ahimsa-abolitionist loving adjustment is the answer to what is necessary for the upward Evolution of Loving Consciousness**. As Shrila Bhaktisiddhanta Saraswati Thakhur said, "Real religion means proper adjustment." "The Left" or "The Right" or "History" is not totally correct, only our Loving God is totally correct.

Isn't it time to take the next step in the Evolution of Consciousness.

To firmly take the STAND of total animal ahimsa/abolitionist respect for cows, as well as following the other 3 main moral principles - no intoxication, no speculative get-something-for-nothing type gambling, and proper marriage; and as the main goal and engagement of life, to always chant and sing and remember God's Glories, and to never forget God.

And now may God show us Absolute Truth and Supreme beauty. All credit for the ideas herein belong to the great souls who have come before.

Thank you very much.

Chapter 33
Laugh, Laugh / No More Tears In Heaven

Please laugh at so-called "life" and the absurd situation we are in, because if we never laugh we will all go crazy. Just see, we are here in this present embodiment for, at the longest time, approximately 100 years max... and that's within eternity? What is 100 years within eternity? That's like infinitely less than one grain of sand out of all the grains of sand cumulatively on every beach, in every country, on every planet, in every solar system, in every universe.

Here's another funny thing - that this funny little spherical planet that we are standing on, is so big it looks and feels like it's a flat plate. That's pretty funny.

Then! .. we don't have one drop of sensory experience of where we came from. Where did we come from? "Oh I came from Chicago."

And then, the equally mysterious question - where are we all going? Where are we all going? LA I think.

God is everywhere and in everything. And simultaneously God is nowhere and in nothing. God is both Supreme Comedian and Supreme Magician. And Supreme Hypnotist.

A great comedian in the eyes of the world, passed away in 2021. But can you believe that God, even when God's standup comedy routine bombs, that God is still infinitely funnier, than the sum total of all the comedians that ever lived?

What's the biggest joke ever told? And who wrote that joke? God wrote it. And what's the joke? ... The one we are living - that this world is the place for our enjoyment, and that we are all materially equal, and additionally that we are all equal to God.

There are so many apparently high ideals and feelings in this world, like love, honor, duty, compassion and so on. Then we tear a chicken's leg off and eat it? Not so funny.

Even holier-than-thou grain and fruit eating vegans are killing and eating thousands and thousands of babies. There's a complete baby embryo plant inside every seed.

But be sure to offer your killings to God. Then God will forgive your killings if you take time to thank God for giving you something to kill, and do it for God's glory? Right? That's pretty funny if you think about it. Okay maybe not so funny.

It's also pretty funny that the train of life is headed for a cliff, and we are busy partying and really trying to enjoy God's property before the sausage train cars drop off into the abyss one by one. Again maybe not so funny but really hilarious from the cartoon character the Roadrunner's, outside perspective.

What else is funny? How about if God were on Twitter how many followers would God have?

But maybe the ultimate funny thing is that the only cure for the constant killing of this thing called life… is death. Die to live.

No More Tears in Heaven. Ha, ha.

Always look for the Absolute Truth and the Supreme Beauty.

And try to laugh once in a while.

Chapter 34
Science Devours Itself

This chapter is taken from the book, *Search for Sri Krishna Reality the Beautiful*, by B. R. Shridhar Maharaj.

"This should be the line of our search; all other inquiries are false. This so-called scientific research is a wild goose chase. It is suicidal.

The atomic [and virus] researchers will soon prove that this kind of science devours itself; it sucks its own blood. It will live, feeding on its own flesh and the flesh of its friends. Material scientific knowledge is no knowledge. We must acquaint ourselves with a vital understanding of pure, real knowledge.

We must absorb ourselves and others in that knowledge, remove darkness and bring light, remove misery and establish [by entering into existing] eternal peace.

Science means not to extend the jurisdiction of exploitation, knowing full well there will be a reaction. By extending the space of exploitation, we will also surely be exploited. If one knowingly commits an offense, then they are charged with more punishment. So, so-called scientific advancement is suicidal.

And it is clearly proven: presently the leading countries of the world are threatening each other with atomic weapons [and man-made viruses], the highest product[s] of the scientists.

What is the difference between the atomic bomb, and the neutron bomb? The neutron bomb [and deadly viruses] are something like a death ray that will kill the people, but will not destroy the buildings.

The neutron bomb will kill all the humans; the houses, and the buildings and everything else will be left behind. The bed will be there, the furniture, everything else will be there, but only the life will be gone, and the bodies will become rotten. That is the effect of the neutron bomb.

And those who emerge victorious will come to enjoy all these things. They will have to remove the dead bodies, and fill the place up with their own people. This is a reaction in the plane of exploitation.

So, this is a suicidal civilization. The whole civilization is rotten to the bottom. They are exploiting nature for the apparent good of human society, but it is incurring a loan from nature that must be paid to the penny with interest.

Because they do not believe this, they will have no relief. They will be forced to clear the debt; nature won't forgive them. Nature is there like a computer, calculating.

So, this civilization is anti-civilization. The whole thing is rotten, a camouflage, a treachery to the soul world. But our policy is different: plain living and high thinking.

Our policy should be to make the best use of a bad bargain. Somehow or other, we have already come here, so now we have to utilize our time and energy in such a way that with the least exploitation we can get out of this material world."

All glory to God. Thank you very much.

Chapter 35
One And A Half Gurus,
And A Life Of Least Exploitation

In the hippie 60's, U.S. Christian preachers warned that Indian guru's coming to the west had a very dangerous philosophy of "Oneness and Equality" with God. And that is true except for at least one and a half Gurus. Be sure to read to the end of this chapter where I will reveal who and how there were one and a half gurus.

The Indian mayavad "Oneness and Equality" idea is attractive, but is only half-truth and therein lies the danger. The full truth is that, more-so than being ONE in EQUALITY with God, or that all ideas, persons and cultures are EQUAL, the full truth is that we are always SERVANTS of God. And the Marxists just say that there is no God.

In the world of exploitation, where we are now, HALF-TRUTH is the chosen method of MANIPULATION, pretty much on every level by every group, every organization, and every individual.

It may be attributed to laziness, or the tendency to jump the gun on limited information, or conscious manipulation, but half-truth is UBER common. When one believes only in the half-truth of EQUALITY with God, or that there is no God, then POWER is the quality of God that seems to be the most sought after.

And when EQUALITY with God, or EQUALITY among all groups and conceptions within this world is the highest goal, then TRUTH takes second place, if it places at all.

So TRUTH is the major casualty of most atheists and Marxists, and also of the incomplete Indian guru teaching of oneness and equality with God, and of oneness and equality of groups, societies, and cultures etcetera.

That we are always SERVANTS of God IS HUMILITY. As SERVANTS of God, we are NOT EQUAL with God. The socialist and communist idea and philosophy is that of altruistic material equality. The fact is we are not equal, so socialism and communism are misinformed ideas. Some tincture of truth is there, but not, the whole truth and nothing but the truth.

In the mid 60's there was one guru that came to the West representing an Indian group called Gaudia Vishnavas who are staunchly opposed to half-truth "oneness and equality" Indians who are the numeric majority of Indians, including now many of the Indian CEOs of the biggest tech companies in the West. That one Guru was A.C. Bhaktivedanta Prabhupada. Shrila Bhaktivedanta Prabhupada was actually preceded in the West in book form by his grandfather guru by the name of Bhaktivinode Thakura whose book *Lord Chaitanya: His Life and Precepts* appeared in England and McGill University in Canada in 1896. So the book form of Bhaktivinode Thakur is the one-half guru mentioned earlier.

India and China are historical long standing enemies of each other but now in the world of modern atheistic globalism, the oneness and equality, big tech controlling Indians in the West are natural brothers and partners with the CCP, the Chinese Communist Party. Add in the foundationally atheistic scientists, and the power intoxicated globalist corporate elites & oligarchs, and their owned mainstream legacy media, and you have what's going on in the material world in 2022.

To sum things up, the philosophies of: "Altruistic oneness, and equality" or that there is no God, both lead to hell.

This material world is the world of domination, always was, always will be. But the spiritual idea is that with the LEAST exploitation we need to get out of this place of mass formation psychosis. Hallelujah and a plant-based vegan, non-mayavad, non-oneness Hare Krishna.

And now may God show us the Truth, the Whole Truth, and Nothing But the Truth.

Thank you very much.

Chapter 36
We Can Worship God
Without Killing Or Stealing From Animals

Thoughtless mentality kills and steals UNNECESSARILY.

WE may STOP killing and eating animals including fish, and stop imprisoning & stealing cow's or other animal's milk or eggs. Eating any kind of animal product is unnecessary. A plant-based diet is prescribed in Genesis 1.29 *AND* in Bhagavad Gita 9.26. Muslims, in addition to following the Quran, also accept the story of the Garden of Eden's pure, original, plant-based diet in the unfallen state. And in the Buddhist Mahayana Mahaparinirvana Sutra - the final teachings of Gautama Buddha - the Buddha effectively prescribes a plant-based, vegan diet.

The PREPONDERANCE of modern scientific evidence prescribes a plant-based diet. And your own childlike pure, sweet, innocent heart should also ultimately prescribe a total plant-based vegan diet for yourself.

There is no excuse for unnecessarily imprisoning and exploiting animals to eat, or to steal and drink their milk, created for THEIR babies.

Necessary and essential fine-brain-tissue promoting vitamin B12, in the recent past mostly only available from animal products and milk, is *now* easily available from non-animal sources. Humans have *no need* for *Stockholm Syndrome* suffering cow's milk. Vitamin B12 supplementation negates any necessity of exploiting and eating any animal products. In this regard I have written a whole paperback book, *Eat Your Way To Health: Healing, Kindness And The Plant Life Cycle*, on all the specifics of the plant-based diet - available by gifting only $20 US via PayPal, including YOUR MAILING ADDRESS, to my email address: mdasa1@gmail.com. Or get the eBook version for only $10 US sent via PayPal, (including your email address for delivery), to my same email address.

I have been vegan for many years and my wife from India is also a long time, healthy-eating, vegan, world-class chef. I hold a Certificate in Plant-based Nutrition from Cornell University and my book, *Eat Your Way To Health: Healing, Kindness And The Plant Life Cycle* has received a five star book review from the former research administrator of the Harvard school of public health; and a glowing testimonial from a Doctor of Education from Boston University, who was also Associate Provost and Dean of Graduate Studies and Professor of Literary Education at the University of Southern Maine.

Give up on siding with the masses, and switch to flying with the angels.

Speaking of flying with angels, get a **free** copy of a finished vector scalable to large sizes without blurring, "GOD FIRST Ahimsa Vegan" logo by simply sending an email directly to my same email address given above, include somewhere in the Subject or body the words - Free Logo.

Being a non-interference, ahimsa/abolitionist VEGAN follower though, is NOT enough, one must preeminently be devoted only to God. Be conscious of God always, and always try to please God by engaging in voluntary, spontaneous loving service to God, mainly by always remembering God and never forgetting God every minute of every day.

But if we are killing, or imprisoning and stealing the milk of a highly conscious *Stockholm Syndrome* suffering domesticated animal - now that we have heard that easily available non-animal source vitamin B12 negates any necessity of eating *any* animal products - if we continue to kill and steal from animals, we are siding with those of faulty mentality and are falling short of our divine potential.

In summary: Always remember God and never forget God, and eat a healthy, SCRIPTURALLY requested, plant-based AHIMSA vegan, UNFALLEN diet.

Thank you very much.

Chapter 37
Where Does Ecstasy Come From?

What is our ultimate situation? We are helplessly cursed – cursed to kill to eat. And worst of all, we enjoy it. How despicable. How helplessly despicable.

Of all things beautiful and noble, killing is not one of them. And we kill constantly. But "Oh, I'm hungry and that gives me the right to kill", and in a fit of hubris we even think, in a way, the right to kill, is like a DUTY to kill something and eat it. Like Holiday feasting is a duty.

And you say, we have no choice but to kill others, because we can't STARVE ourselves. We think we have an inalienable right to kill, and therefore there is no problem in killing, and we don't give it a second thought about the killing part, except to thank God for giving us enough to kill everyday. Duh, that's the curse baby. No choice but to kill, and we don't think twice, that's the curse.

What is the solution to the curse? Many people say the solution is to offer everything we eat to God and then God will absorb the reaction to the curse. Just like Jesus absorbing our sins by dying on a cross. Offering your killings to God is like Jesus dying on the cross. Both involve God absorbing the reactions to our sins, as if it's God's fault we kill all the time and that God has to make up for our failing if only we believe something. At some level these things may be true, but I have heard that we need to dive really deep to reach the peak of surrender.

The peak of surrender is for us to heroically accept the results of our actions, not by transferring responsibility to God or to God's servant son, but by acknowledging that

OUR despicableness results from OUR original choice to leave God's company by wanting to be God. And always being aware that we are helplessly despicable right up till our dying day. And then we have a chance to stop disturbing others.

So yes, we are in a cursed position – within this material world of constant interruptions to have to go kill some other body to sustain our temporary body. And in a cursed position of having senses that spend countless hours studying and learning how to scientifically increase our capacity to exploit the resources of God's created nature for our temporary sense pleasure while being connected to a material body. Did I say despicable?

Go ahead and offer all your food to God and then eat what God leaves for you. But always humbly remember that we cursed ourselves, by originally rejecting God. And that the only way out now is to die to live.

But where is the joy, the Ecstasy, the pleasure and the happiness of creation? That is within God and does not come from us. Within God is everything and the highest thing is beauty and ecstasy. Connecting back with God is the only hope of tasting a drop of that eternal ecstasy. But God is not cheap and requires more than we have, so that is why even vegans need God's MERCY at the time of death. Even asking God for mercy is a bit presumptuous, but what else can we do?

And now may God show us the Truth, the Whole Truth, and Nothing but the Truth.

Thank you very much.

Chapter 38
To WANT To Go Home

Hope all is WELL with you. As you all may know, this material world is full of the good *and* the bad. God and God's beauty is the good, and pretty much everything else is the bad.

But to really go home, as Dorothy in the Wizard of Oz wanted to do, we have to find a way out of here.

To go home, first of all, we have got to WANT out. Deeply want to go home. A surface "want out" keeps us here. A sporadic "want out" keeps us here. A tomorrow "want out" keeps us here.

"I want out of the nightmare, completely, forever, PERIOD. I never want to come back here. This is the only thing I want. I want out, to go home, and what others want is their business."

If we are not ALWAYS thinking like this, then we're not ready. We are living in an illusion. We may go to the church, or the temple, or to whatever on Sunday, or everyday, but that is secondary (going to the house of the Lord / Temple may be helpful but it is still secondary, nonetheless). The primary thing is our moment to moment consciousness. What we are thinking about. What we want.

Here is a quote from singer/songwriter Bob Dylan: "There must be some kind of way out of here, said the joker to the thief."

Well, Here's the good news: **There is a way out!**

WANTING out is the way out. Focus on, serve and praise the Creator, as the Supreme Person, not the Creation per se. Pray to God for Mercy, beg God for Mercy, cry to God for Mercy. We are everyday killers of at least plants, and unseen insects etc., with nary a second thought. We need God's Mercy.

We are all in this hellish place together. War after war, deranged attack after deranged attack, constant killing to eat.

If we are REALLY seeing this and feeling this, we would WANT to get out of the material world and go home, and not continue the fairy-tale illusion the marketers want us to believe.

If we WANT out, death is not FORCING us out. Death is Mercy.

What happens to us and what's in store for us is God's business, not our own. "Whatever God wants is all right with me."

The World keeps promising peace, keeps promising peace, but there is no peace. There will never be any peace in this world. Get over it. Grow up and get out of here at least mentally. More song lyrics come to mind like: "... If it's the last thing we ever do."

Until that glorious day when God calls us home - as the way of LEAST EXPLOITATION in this world while we are here - be a God first plant-based vegan and sing the glories of the Lord and of God's Land of Pure Love, and be happy.

My friends, may God show us Absolute Truth and Supreme Beauty. Thank you very much.

Chapter 39
We Are Not These Bodies
And Whole Food Vegan Is Crystal Clear

We are not these bodies. But we are the spiritual spark drivers of these bodies, and we have a choice to make: to drive for either our own temporary bodily and family sense gratification, or to drive for Eternal, Beautiful, Creator-and-Owner God's glory and pleasure.

Krishna, meaning All-Attractive God, is a bona fide name, some say the top name, for the Beautiful plant-based vegan-requesting, Creator God of *both* Genesis 1.29 and Bhagavad Gita 9.26.

Any sincere name for the one loving God will do, but many people in India and now around the world dance and sing for the glory of the beautiful name for God fashioned as Krishna of the Bhagavad Gita. And Krishna indeed is the happy pastoral God who wears a peacock feather in his hair and plays a flute. And is simultaneously bashful and BOLD.

On a related note, life in this world is never settled. One day happiness, the next day distress.

It is God's mercy that we even eat every day. Historically, and even now in a few places, food supply was not easily available.

It is nothing less than miraculous that countless BILLIONS of living entities are eating, and thus killing most every single day.

This killing to eat business, and making babies business, that's pretty much the material world. Virtually all activities are somehow related to these two things.

So eating is connected with maybe half of everything anyone does. It's a big deal, what you eat. A BIG deal.

It's not minor, not a minor thing.

For those who eat animal-free for health reasons, not exploiting animals may be a secondary consideration, but for a committed, let's say a committed animal-dignity Vegan, for an animal-dignity Vegan – at least for myself – the idea of an animal-free diet, thought about with compassionate consideration, is very important to say the least.

And in fact it's not coming from me it's coming from God. In both Genesis 1.29 and in Bhagavad Gita 9.26 God is the originator of the vegan diet. God is God so God can do anything. But God in Scripture, now backed by the preponderance of scientific plant-based nutrition evidence, God everywhere has made it crystal clear that God wants us to follow a plant-based vegan diet. Chant God's holy name, be vegan as per God's request, and be happy.

May God show us the truth, the whole truth, and nothing but the truth.

Namaste, Amen, and thank you very much.

Chapter 40
"The Free Flow Of The Absolute"

From the book, Sermons Of The Guardian Of Devotion, Volume Four, Chapter 2, "The free flow of the Absolute", by B.R. Shridhar Maharaj.

"I must feel that I am unsatisfied with the environment of this world: life, death, torture and all these things. If one is really a sincere seeker of a happy life, then one must try with their utmost endeavor to get free from this environment, and to find another place - home. Back to God, back to home. And we were told from ancient times that we have got a home, and that that home is under the cooling shade of the holy feet of our Lord.

Practically, we must take into our program, and in our daily schedule, wholesale, how to get out of this nasty colony and go back to our home, sweet home. And why is it sweet? We are to discuss that with our intellect. Although intellect is not qualified to know about that, but still in the negative way also we can calculate what the positive is there. In that plane they are eager to take us in. They are honest. So we want to live in that plain as our country because they are honest. There it is infinite, and no population will be suppressed there.

This plane here of constant killing, is not worth living in, so we must search for a place worth living in. And in the quest for that land we may pass lives after lives. In this SEARCH there is no loss because, where we are at present is undesirable, and if we are sincere in this feeling, then to search for what is desirable it's NOT madness. We may pass lives after lives in search of a sweet home, and there will be no waste of time in that endeavor. This is not unreasonable, rather, we find that it is FINELY reasonable.

First is revealed scripture, the positive contribution. Then next, and subservient, is reason. Logic and reason are helpful but subservient, and the POSITIVE EXTENSION from the world of truth, is the REAL THING. God and Absolute Truth are the main things, and logic will be subservient: by the logic of this domain we cannot KNOW anything about the transcendental realm.

Logic may be applied here, but the logic of chemistry may not work in the logic of theology wholesale. Everything has got its own logic. The transcendental world has got its own logic, but this mundane logic may help us partially, as an analogy.

Knowledge is infinite, every unit is infinite. Infinite minus infinite, equals infinite! So the Infinite World is such that we are always in a relative position in the infinite. Infinite can never be finished. Everywhere there is CENTER, nowhere is CIRCUMFERENCE."

You have just read from the book, *Sermons of the Guardian of Devotion, Volume Four*, Chapter 2 titled: "The free flow of the Absolute", by B.R. Shridhar Maharaj.

And now may God show all of us Absolute Truth and Supreme Beauty.

Thank you very much.

Chapter 41
The Mother Of All Elephants In The Room And Where We Go From Here

This chapter is taken and repeated from the Introduction of this book.

This book is a compilation of short essays rendered as chapters, related to Eternal Beautiful God and to the ultimate elephant of all elephants in the material room. Some essays are directly to the point and some are auxiliary, but all contribute to the whole. This compilation book then ends with a summary epilogue, and a wish for humanity.

"Elephant in the room" means something so big you don't see it, or that you don't want to see it because it destroys your preconceived false narrative. So you ignore it.

How can we talk or think of any PERFECTION of a societal utopia (progressive, conservative, or whatever) on earth, when the big elephant in the room, unavoidable *killing to eat*, is negating and erasing EVERY aspiration for real goodness in this world.

This place is, right here and right now the classic hell we imagine, the place of constant killing by everyone, all species.

BUT beyond the door and over the rainbow, there is a place without material killing. All the high concepts have and must have an origin. They do exist, but they do not exist in reality in the material world. But they do beautifully exist in God's spiritual world. And God's abode is not this material world, but is our destination AFTER we are released from this material prison where big mad elephants roam in the room.

And God's abode is so beautiful - so beautiful. And why is God's abode so beautiful, because God is so beautiful.

By hearing from my Spiritual Master, B.R. Shridhar I understand that there exists power, consciousness and superconsciousness, but plain consciousness and existence by itself is dry. Higher than consciousness is the NECESSITY of consciousness, which is beauty and ecstasy.

So when we speak of fulfillment and beauty we are looking for the highest concept of beauty in the Supreme Personality of God. God the father is great, God the son is great, God the merciful is great. But God the ALL-Attractive, is the greatest. God simultaneously at the CENTER of ALL loving relationships is greatest.

God in highest ecstasy is the coming-of-age, teenage God, who lives village life in God's transcendental beautiful rural nature, where playful God is the exclusive talk of the town, NOT in any limited lower mundane sense, but in the highest pure spiritual sense only possible with God proper.

All things good and bad are inconceivably harmonized in God. And being God, God can do anything and everything. But since WE are NOT God, but we are servants of God, we are only to do what God wants us to do. How are we to know what God wants us to do? Scripture, guru and saint POINT the direction, but the guru WITHIN is not to be neglected.

Eating entails disturbance to, stealing from, killing and grinding with our teeth, swallowing and passing out other fellow living entities. It's not that we have to stop eating, but to do that we will have to wait patiently until we are called home by God.

So we are going to the place where we don't kill to eat. And until God calls us home and gives us passage through the door and over the rainbow, if we are civilized we are to live in this world following the full ahimsa vegan principle of doing the LEAST EXPLOITATION of others. And that LEAST EXPLOITATION is premised on 100% plant-based, ahimsa vegan worship of God the ALL-ATTRACTIVE Personality.

A note here is that the name for God, Krishna, means "All-Attractive God". But as God is Absolute, all names for God are equal as names of God. So please, **no fighting about the particular name for God!**

In summary:

GOD IS ALL-ATTRACTIVE and

The ultimate elephant in the material room is:
KILLING TO MAINTAIN EXISTENCE

So, what to do?

Again, we are to worship God, and as the least exploitation while in this material world of constant killing, we are to follow a healthy whole-food ahimsa vegan, 100% plant-based diet as per Genesis 1.29 and Bhagavad Gita 9.26, which is now also prescribed by the preponderance of modern scientific evidence. Full Circle. Can't we see it? Full Circle. God knows the past, present and future. Always did - always will.

Chapter 42
Vegan Krishna Or Krishna Vegan

Vegan Krishna, or Krishna Vegan, the point is, God, by the name Krishna in Bhagavad Gita, which Gita, or song of God, belongs to the whole world especially now in the age of the internet - the ultimate Creator God of beauty, love and affection, and of selfless service, God who knows everything past, present and future, although appearing at a specific time and place in the world's history namely 5,000 years ago, knew then and knows now that the created souls of this world need to pass thru this embodied life with the LEAST amount of nasty exploitation. This idea is known as ahimsa.

The two questions are: 1. Can our knowledge of the least amount of exploitation, positively evolve forward over time, and 2. Exactly what is the least amount of exploitation?

Evolution of consciousness is more important than evolution of bodily form or evolution of technology, because in the absence of evolution of consciousness, evolution of technology is suicidal, witness nuclear bombs and laboratory-created deadly viruses. So evolution of consciousness is the thing.

The cows that Krishna appeared with in this world, are not the cows of this world. Those SURABHI cows were totally spiritual in form. Because all animals value their freedom just like we value our freedom, the cows of this world, in any form or situation, in view of the *evolved* Ahimsa principal, and especially in view of new knowledge of how the necessary "fine brain and nerve tissue" promoting vitamin B12 in mother cow's milk, which can today be

.obtained without extracting milk from captured and gender exploited prisoner cows; the cows of this material world should not be owned and controlled by human beings, but should be wild and free just like all animals. This can be done simply by not breeding them in captivity. "Protected" is not free. Indians were "protected" by the British. So in maturity, protection is not the thing, *freedom* is the thing.

In view of both Genesis 1.29, fruits and herbs; and Bhagavad Gita 9.26 a leaf, a flower, fruit and WATER, Vegan Krishna means that God has already told us the evolved idea of minimum exploitation while in this world of birth, killing, and eventual personal death, which personal death ironically ends all nasty killing to eat, and ends exploitation of others less powerful than us, including plants. The least exploitation in this world necessarily includes completely following a whole-food, plant-only diet.

Worship God, follow a 100% plant-based ahimsa vegan diet, and pray for God's mercy, whatever God decides that mercy is, at the time of our death.

And now may God show everyone Absolute Truth and Supreme Beauty.

Namaste, shalom, salaam, and thank you very much.

Chapter 43
Krishna Vegan Is Evergreen

The ideas talked about in this book are mostly what are called evergreen, meaning they are always true and are generally not current events and ideas that change moment by moment.

We want to live in ahimsa vegan eternity and not in this temporary material world. While embodied in this temporary material world because of our misguided desires, we should do the minimum exploitation necessary to pass through this place, while we dovetail our full internal consciousness with things that are permanent and that do not change season by season or year by year.

Factual, as it really is, this is why we know Krishna is a bona fide name for our bona fide loving God of many names, because what Krishna said 5000 years ago about diet in Bhagavad Gita was true then, although misinterpreted, and remains true now. Now it can be clearly seen that what Krishna prescribed in Bhagavad Gita to offer God is our proper diet: a leaf, a flower, fruit and water. No animals, no milk. Which is the same as prescribed in Genesis, the first book of the Judeo/Christian bible. The story of the pure Garden of Eden is also accepted by the Muslem Faith.

The goal of this book is to find and bring together like-minded individuals who catch and are committed to the understanding that God in Bhagavad Gita and the same God in pre-fallen Genesis, in both scriptures, prescribed an animal free diet for humans on this planet, and that our calling is to think of and worship God constantly while eating a minimalist, and healthy 100% plant-based diet, and to set the poor cows free simply by not breeding them in captivity. Problem solved in one bovine generation.

We don't want Hindu vegans, or Christian vegans, or Muslim vegans or atheist vegans, we want just plain vegans that want to love God with all their heart, by ANY name for our LOVING, SWEET GOD who is inconceivably, simultaneously, everywhere and nowhere at the same time.

If you fall in this like-minded group - that we are to constantly remember and worship God and that we can now see that God prescribed an animal-free diet for humans in both Genesis 1.29, and in Bhagavad Gita 9.26 - if you fall in this highly evolved group and want to connect with other like-minded individuals world-wide, please send a "Yes, God is great." email to mdasa1@gmail.com and I will attempt to establish personal & friendly connections between us all. There is strength and encouragement in numbers. We are made to individually love God, but also to congregationally worship and praise God.

Your email information will NOT be used for any money requests or to try to sell you anything.

Again, to connect with like-minded, dairy-free, internally full-time devotees of God, send an email to mdasa1@gmail.com and if God wills we will build a worldwide community of truly God-loving free and compassionate persons.

Respects. Thank you very much.

Chapter 44
Free Logo - "GOD FIRST Ahimsa Vegan"

As a free service to faithful readers, we have designed and produced a "GOD FIRST, Ahimsa Vegan" logo in a vector image format that can be printed and resized without losing sharpness.

To order your FREE logo please send an email to mdasa1@gmail.com with the words Free Logo in the Subject line or body of the email.

What our hearts are trying to find, pure & lasting ecstasy, real beauty, and real love and charm, is not located here in this world, because here, we and everyone else are constant killers.

But it does come from somewhere, so it's got to be on the other side, beyond the door.

In the meantime God by scriptural authority, by scientific authority, *and* by the authority of your own heart, God wants us to grow up and at least wean ourselves from killing animals and stealing their baby's milk. God prescribes a plant-based diet in both Genesis 1.29 and Bhagavad Gita 9.26.

Reality and purity live beyond this world and they exist by themselves and for themselves. In Vedic traditional culture they are Radha-Krishna, and the Divine Couple by many other names.

Heaven is definitely not here on this planet. That's actually good news. Because this place is a really dead-end place in so many ways.

Hope is a great thing. Otherwise what would there be here?

The great virtues are negated in this world by the fact that everybody kills and eats others every day so that they can stay here.

As per action and reaction, we ALL deserve to die, to be erased. One group says that we can avoid being erased by believing that God paid the penalty for our sins. Why should God pay the penalty? Why not WE go willingly and humbly to God and let God do with us as God wills. And pray that God is merciful on us. But better than that is to forget about ourselves and focus on God's Supreme Beauty and Eternality.

And now, may God show all of us God's causeless mercy and don't forget to send that email to order your free "GOD FIRST, Ahimsa Vegan" logo.

Thank you very much.

Chapter 45
Duty To Serve God

Fallen means desire to dominate, to enjoy rather than to serve. Dominate rather than harmonize. Like Satan said in the Garden of Eden, to have knowledge equal to God. You will be like God. Effectively a Declaration of Independence from God. "I decide what is good and evil." You will be like God. Yea right! We have all chosen to dominate, but then we lose because we can't stop our own impending death.

The effect of choosing the path of dominance, is to become subconsciously self-conscious of being unprotected and alone, which is the fact & which causes constant internal gnawing fear. To cover that gnawing fear so many take to intoxication - either via drugs or by addictively striving for attainment of power dominance.

Because of the original desire to dominate, known in the Judeo/Christian/Muslim world as Original Sin, we have entered this world of constant killing to eat that never stops. This means all so-called "living" species are constant dominators that never stop dominating. So, as long as we are embodied, we are in the fallen dominating condition.

Cooperation and harmony with God, is to bow to God's requests. Your mission should you decide to accept is to constantly strive, to minimize exploitation and dominance on our journey to death, on our journey back home to God. Death means to dominate no more. Surrendered loving acceptance of death, is to love God.

A Godly life is to not dominate. Death is the doorway to actual Godly life. By loving God and accepting God's solution and decision in death, the *goal* of life is accomplished. Die to live. How do you like them apples?

Only God has ALL rights and privileges. God wants us to CHOSE not to dominate against God's requests of us. What are God's requests of us? In the West the Ten Commandments come to mind. Of them, the one that bears investigation and reflection is "Thou shall NOT kill."

That's the one where God indirectly is telling us OUR bodily death is what God requires for us to please God, because as long as we are embodied we kill. Well done my faithful servant, to see that DEATH is the returning back home to the place of NO killing. "Free at last, thank God Almighty we are free at last."

The desire to dominate and control others is manifest in most positions of power over others, whereby influencers, controllers, leaders, etc., have a higher status; and pecking-order-wise get to dominate others. And every entity & human that eats is manifesting dominance. *This* material world is the world of the desire to dominate.

SERVICE to GOD is the opposite of dominance. Our service to God is preceded & guided by those that have come before us. We owe everything to God and we owe others who have come before us and help us in our journey back home to Godhead. Owing everything to God and to others - that is our duty to serve.

And now may God show us the *Almighty* Truth and Supreme Beauty.

Thank you for reading. I pray you are all doing well in your evolving conscious journey, back home, back to Godhead.

Epilogue

Our duty as human beings is to always remember God, and never forget God. Animals and human beings all eat, sleep, mate and defend. Highest calling human beings self-restrain and minimize animal bodily activities to always remember God.

A final wish for humanity - May we ALWAYS remember God because that accomplishes & encompasses everything we are created to do. If we do that we will surely be:

Flying With Angels GOD FIRST

Keyword Index

Abolitionist	- 6x2, 20, 31, 62, 66, 88x2, 110, 111x2, 139
Ahimsa	- 5, 9x2, 11, 13x2, 16, 20, 23, 27, 61x2, 62, 66, 67, 72x2, 73x2, 74, 84, 110x2, 111x2, 131x2, 132x2, 134, 136x2, 137, 139x3, 143x2,, 144
Birth	- 13, 14, 54x2, 55, 57x3, 60, 66, 75, 79, 85, 86x2, 133
Chant	- 26, 42, 66x2, 67, 71x2, 92, 98x2, 99, 110, 111, 126
Consciousness	- 8x5, 16, 17, 18, 30, 32, 42, 44x2, 45, 55, 57, 60, 61, 63x2, 78, 89, 110x2, 111x2, 123, 130x5, 132x3, 134
Death	- Contents, 11x3, 14x4, 15x4, 16x2, 19x2, 23x2, 27x2, 29, 30x5, 31x3, 32, 34x2, 35x3, 36x2, 38, 41, 47, 48x2, 53, 54x5, 55x5, 57x9, 60, 66x2, 75, 78, 79x4, 80, 81, 83, 85x5, 86x6, 89, 90, 98, 103x2, 113, 114, 119x6, 120x2,122, 124x2, 127, 133x3
Equality	- 21, 40, 66, 105, 106x6, 116x8, 117x4
Eternity	- Contents, 11x4, 12x3, 13, 16, 17, 21, 22, 23, 27x2, 28x2, 37, 38, 47, 64x2, 81x2, 110, 112x2, 134
Evolution	- Testimonials, 45, 61, 73, 89x4, 110, 111x2, 132x6
Guru	- 5, 6, 19x2, 11, 44, 45x3, 75, 116x5, 117x4, 130x2, 143
Happiness	- Contents, 17x3, 29, 48x3, 49, 66x3, 80, 81x2, 122, 125
Hitler	- 57, 60
Holy Name	- 13, 18, 26, 35, 38, 58, 66x2, 72, 97, 98x2, 99, 103, 104x2, 110x4, 126
India	- 60, 70, 73x4, 74x2, 84, 106x5, 116x3, 117x6, 125, 139, 143x2
ISKCON	- 79
Krishna	- 5x2, 6, 9x, 45, 55, 59, 76, 91, 97x3, 110, 114, 118, 125x3, 131, 132x6, 133, 134x4, 136
Life	- 5x2, 6, 9x2, 12, 15x3, 16, 24x5, 30x4, 32x9, 33x10, 34x6, 35x6, 42, 47, 48x4, 50, 51x2, 52, 54, 57, 61, 72, 79, 84, 85x4, 86x2, 88, 89x3, 92x2, 93, 94, 97, 98x8, 100x3, 104, 109x2, 110x3, 111, 112, 113x2, 115, 116, 117, 119x3, 125, 127x2, 130, 132, 138, 143
Oneness	- 40x2, 106x5, 107, 116x4, 117x3, 118
Peace	- Testimonials, 5, 6, 20x2, 34, 42, 43, 46, 52, 61, 62, 63, 79x2, 80x4, 81x4, 82x3, 88, 101, 109, 110, 114, 124x4
Prabhupada	- 55, 79, 117x2, 143
Religion	- 6, 11x2, 44, 73, 76, 92, 108, 109, 111
Service	- Testimonials-x2, 24, 65, 92x8, 100x2, 101, 105, 120x2, 132, 136, 139
STOCKHOLM	- 66x2, 84, 88, 97, 102x2, 110, 138, 139
Suffering	- 29, 53, 66x2, 67x2, 84, 88, 97, 102, 110, 138, 139
War	- 33, 39, 42x2, 54, 55, 59, 60x4, 88, 102, 116, 124x2

About the Author:

Madhava Das also known as "Dasa", is the retired Founder & President of Nutritional Research Maui and holds a Cornell University Certificate in Plant-Based Nutrition.

As a young man Dasa suffered from chronic lung congestion and extremely high blood pressure. Both of Dasa's parents died young from chronic degenerative diseases. That inspired Dasa to deeply study healthy eating, and the result of that study was his first perceptive book, *Eat Your Way to Health: Healing, Kindness And The Plant Life Cycle*.

Along the way Dasa was a founder of the sport of hang gliding, and contributed to the design of the Gossamer Condor, the first successful human powered aircraft, now hanging at the Smithsonian Air And Space Museum in Washington, D.C. beside the Original Wright Brothers Flyer and the Apollo 11 Command Module, Columbia, that took the first humans to walk on the moon.

Dasa traveled to India many times and received Gaudiya Vaishnava first and second spiritual initiation from His Divine Grace Shrila B. R. Shridhar Maharaj, the highly qualified and dearmost confidential Godbrother, shiksha guru, and friend of His Divine Grace Shrila Bhaktivedanta Swami Prabhupada.

India is the source of sanatana dharma ahimsa *vegetarianism*, and is poised to be the future leader of sanatana dharma ahimsa *veganism*.

Madhava Dasa of Maui, Hawaii has a history of leading-edge thought in multiple fields, and is at the present time the leading proponent of GOD FIRST Ahimsa Vegan thought that recognizes that the spiritual abode is the only place without killing to live. In other words we only stop killing when we leave our mortal bodies & enter into God's peacock and parrot populated garden playground.

Copyright © 2022 Madhava Dasa

145 Dasa/Flying With Angels

www.ingramcontent.com/pod-product-compliance
Lightning Source LLC
Chambersburg PA
CBHW070813100426
42742CB00012B/2351